THE ANGEL AND THE ANTS

The Angel and the Ants

Bringing Heaven Closer to Your Daily Life

Peter Kreeft

Servant Publications
Ann Arbor, Michigan

Charis Books is an imprint of Servant Publications especially designed to serve Roman Catholics.

Published by Servant Publications
P.O. Box 8617
Ann Arbor, Michigan 48107

Cover and text design by Diane Bareis

95 96 97 98 10 9 8 7 6 5 4 3

Printed in the United States of America
ISBN 0-89283-881-7

Library of Congress Cataloging-in-Publication Data

Kreeft, Peter.
The angel and the ants : bringing heaven closer to your daily life / Peter Kreeft
p. cm.
"Charis books."
ISBN 0-89283-881-7
1. Christian life–Catholic authors. 2. Heaven–Christianity. 3. God–Love. 4. Prayer–Christianity. 5. Suffering–Religious aspects–Christianity. I. Title
BX2350.2.K67 1994
242–dc20 94-25061
CIP

Contents

Introduction

The title of this book, taken from one of its chapters, sounds very strange. Is it a book about angels, ants, or both?

Neither. It is a book about us, but in the vertical relationship, the upward look, the heavenward road.

Until recently, everyone knew reality was a vertical hierarchy, a ladder, with matter at the bottom, then plants, then animals, then humans, then angels, then God at the top. This was not ideology or theology but common sense and simple sanity.

Today both scholars and ordinary sane human beings seriously claim to believe that animals have rights like people, or even that animals *are* people, or that people are mere animals, or have no more rights than animals–or even fewer, if the people are unwanted unborn babies and the animals are endangered species. ("Be a hero, save a whale; save a baby, go to jail.") The hierarchy has been toppled. The totem pole is cut down, and even God is cut down to our level, as a Chum, or a Process, or a mere "man-for-others," or a Force.

Augustine and Pascal both said that there were two mistakes we could make about ourselves: to confuse ourselves with animals and to confuse ourselves with angels, or gods, or God himself. Some contemporary thinkers seem to have managed to pull off both of those human heresies at the same time.

Our relationship with God is vertical. Our fundamental response to God, if we are sane and live in the real world, is worship, adoration. "I fell at his feet as one dead"–that is how the prophet speaks when he meets the real God.

God is infinitely farther above us than we are above ants; farther than angels are above ants. We are far less than ants compared to God. We are infinitely precious, but we are infinitely precious sub-ants.

Only on this presupposition is it wonderful that God has raised us, through Christ, to share his own nature (2 Pt 1:4). It is more wonderful than an ant becoming an angel.

That is what this book is about: the wonder of the God-relationship, as it works out in our daily prayer and practice. It's about the love-relationship, the intimacy, the spiritual marriage, that we have entered into if we are Christians, especially if we are Catholics (though 99 percent of the things in this book are for biblical Protestants too).

Its chapters are self-contained and (usually) short, so that they can be read over a single cup of coffee, or used for a single meditation. As anyone will see who is at all far advanced in this life, it is a book by a beginner for other beginners.

PART ONE

Beginnings

ONE

The First Thing

What's the most sought-after topic for religious workshops, articles, columns, talks, and books, time after time, place after place? It's always how to pray, how to be a saint, how to love God.

This proves two things. 1) This thirst, the thirst not just to know *about* God but to *know* God, is unchangeable and innate in the human heart. 2) This thirst is not finding living water in our society, not even our religious society.

This chapter will be about The First Thing, "the one thing necessary" (Lk 10:42). That thing has often been called by put-off names like "spirituality," or "the spiritual life," or "the inner life." The thing is simply knowing God, intimacy with God, the "and" in "He and I."

I want to take up questions like these: Why can't we find time to pray? Why don't recommended methods seem to work? Why isn't prayer escapist and selfish? How is it connected to social action? Why aren't we all saints? Can we do anything to become saints? What did the saints do to become saints? Is prayer the same as meditation? Are the two contradictory or complementary? Is there a special kind of prayer or a special kind of sanctity for busy people? How can we learn to find God everywhere and everywhen?

Life offers only two absolute values—knowledge and love. It offers only three inexhaustible objects for these values—yourself, your neighbor, and God. This means that life has six ultimate purposes: knowing yourself, loving yourself, knowing your neighbor, loving your neighbor, knowing God, and loving God. These six purposes are so ultimate that they are the only ones that carry over into eternity. They are what we are designed to do forever. So we'd better learn to practice well here.

As Shakespeare's mind holds the secret of Hamlet's identity, so the God who designed us holds the secret of our true identity. Therefore we cannot know ourselves or our neighbors rightly except in knowing him. And we cannot love rightly without knowing rightly.

Thomas Merton wrote many profound sentences. I think this was the profoundest—and the simplest: "We are not at peace with others because we are not at peace with ourselves, and we are not at peace with ourselves because we are not at peace with God."

This explains the origin of all war and all neurosis. Politics depends on psychology, and psychology depends on religion.

Religion, in turn, depends on sanctity. Without living contact with God, without knowing and loving God, religion is a sham and a shell, churches and seminaries empty out, and so do hearts and lives. In other words, modern times.

Nature abhors a vacuum. So to fill the religious vacuum, social action enterprises that are indistinguishable from secular ones come in, together with a vague hope that a heavenly benevolence will smile its approval. Contrast this with the staple diet of all the saints: the alarming and passionate awareness of a spiritual warfare and a supernatural love affair with God.

I will never forget a line I read in a book by an ex-Christian who became a Zen Buddhist: "I could find books and teachers who told me what the doctrine was, but I could not find anyone who experienced the doctrine." He didn't find experience among Christians. When he found it among Buddhists, he became one.

The line has haunted me. I write not to help others become Buddhists, but to help them become Christians.

But what right do I have to write for such a purpose? Am I an "expert" myself on loving God? If I say yes, I am a fool, a Pharisee, and a liar. If I say no, I am a useless teacher—or so it seems.

My answer is a clear no—I am no expert on loving God. But I may still hope to say something useful, because there are two different kinds of useful teachers. The first is the expert who speaks from the mountaintop to us scrabblers in the brush below. The second is a fellow scrabbler.

Books written from the mountaintop are readily available to Catholics. They are the books of the saints—Augustine, Aquinas, Francis, Bernard, Bonaventure, Teresa of Avila, Thérèse of Lisieux, and John of the Cross—the Doctors of the Church. By all means go to them. They are gold.

I can't even honestly say, "Go to them first, then come to me," for I can't say come to me at all. All I can do is share my experience with you. And it will be mainly experience of failure, not success. But we can all learn from our failures. I suppose that's why God permits us to have so many.

Loving God is an art, not a science (at one extreme) or an instinctive knack (at the other extreme). It isn't a mechanical technique like engineering that can be taught perfectly. Neither is it an innate ability like walking that can't be taught at all. It *can* be taught, but only from friend to friend.

So this book is written to you as a friend. As you read, imagine yourself in conversation with me, as we both rush in where angels fear to tread, through the brambles of the foothills (perhaps only the anthills) of the holy mountain of God.

TWO

God and Me

"God and me"—it seems terribly exclusive, private, even selfish. Hardly Christian. Christianity isn't "God and me"; it's God, ***my neighbors***, and me. An individualistic Christianity of "God and me" is not the Christianity of Christ. So the objection might go.

The objector might add that even if "God and me" ***was*** acceptable in the past, it cannot be today. We live in a global village; essential social concerns press upon all of us. The church says so too; most of the great papal encyclicals during the past hundred years have been ***social*** encyclicals.

"God and me" Christianity comes not from Christ but from Augustine, the objector might go on to say. Augustine writes the following dialogue between God and his soul:

God: What would you know?
Soul: Just two things.
God: State them.
Soul: Who you are, and who I am.
God: Nothing more?
Soul: Nothing more.

But St. Paul has something more: a social Christianity in which we are "members of one another" (Rom 12:5) and a cosmic Christianity in which "the whole creation groans and travails with us" (Rom 8:22).

So why "God and me?"

Because it's authentically Christian. Christ centered first on the "God and me" relationship. He came to die to restore it. He related to people always one at a time, not as classes or masses. He was first of all a savior, not a social worker. The same is true of all the saints: though they did not neglect social issues (even the hermit left the world in order to pray for it), yet they all began with and centered on the relationship between themselves and God. For they were disciples of the master who taught, "What does it profit a man if he gains the whole world and loses his own soul?" (Mt 16:26). First things first.

A dualism or opposition between "God and me" and social concerns is taught *not* by traditional "God and me" Christians, but by their liberal critics, modernistic or socialistic Christians. In traditional Christianity, the vertical "God and me" relationship and the horizontal "me and others" relationship are the two bars of the same cross.

The supposed opposition is a false one for two reasons: first, the only adequate foundation for social action is personal sanctity; and second, genuine sanctity always issues in social responsibility.

Let's look more closely at these two points.

1. There are two competing versions of the good society, depending on where you locate the source of good and evil: in hearts or in social programs and institutions. Christianity, like nearly all pre-modern social philosophies, believes the first. How could you make a good society without good people? How could you make a good brick wall without good bricks? Modern liberalism, stemming from Hobbes, Locke, Rousseau, Mill, and Marx, trusts in society or institutions to make good people.

Take the problem of war. James 4 says that the origin of

physical war in society is spiritual war in individuals. Therefore the most effective social action to eliminate war must begin with peace in individual hearts. There is no peace with others until there is peace with ourselves and with God.

History confirms this: Saints have changed the world more than states have. Slavery was abolished from states only after it was abolished from hearts.

2. The other side of the coin is that true sanctity always reaches out to others. There is no danger in "God and me," for God will always send me to you. But there is a danger in "you and me," because you will not necessarily send me to God.

   Some saints entered politics. Most did not. But even those who did not, exercised mighty acts of private, *concrete* charity.

   Christ never told us to love humanity or society. But he commanded us to love our *neighbor*.

Separating personal sanctity and social action (private or public) is like separating faith and works, or justification and sanctification, or the first and second table of the Law.

But we must *understand* this objection, not just *refute* it. What is its origin?

Its origin is with the enemies of Christianity. They created the false dualism as propaganda, and they have sold it to many naïve Christians through their control of the media, which regularly caricatures "God and me" Christians as bigots, fools, and idiots.

Its origin is with the liberal religion of social salvation without personal salvation or morality—a false religion that hates and fears the true religion of Christ because its demand for detachment from the world and its sexual morality threaten modernity's two most cherished addictions: greed and lust.

The origin of the opposition between "God and me" and social concern, the origin of the objection against "God and me," is not the church but the enemies of the church and of Christ and of your eternal soul.

THREE

Lesson One

Let's compare two sets of words:

1. Progressive, advanced, sophisticated, nuanced, adult, complex.
2. Simplistic, naïve, childish, fanatical, simple-minded, black-and-white, cut-and-dried, dogmatic.

Now let's ask two questions about them:

1. Which set of words do our culture's "experts" use as words of praise, and which of blame?
2. Would Jesus Christ agree or disagree?

Jesus never said that the way to his kingdom was "adult" or "sophisticated." What he did say was: "Unless you turn [change] and become like little children, you cannot enter the kingdom of heaven."

Please consider that one sentence slowly, thoughtfully, honestly, and without prejudice for one full minute before reading any further. Notice each word carefully, for Infinite Wisdom chooses his words with infinite care.

Are you back?

All I can add to that is a P.S. or a commentary, which is not original but is a summary of the fundamental teaching of all the saints, based on their experience, not just mine, beginning with the greatest saint who ever lived, Mary.

Let's lay it out step by step.

1. Life, however complex it is (and in our day it is indeed complex in many ways), is fundamentally simple. It is like a teepee, or a pyramid: it comes to a point. It has a point.

2. That point is its purpose, its end, its design, its goal. Life is designed by an intelligence; therefore, like a work of art, it has a unity of end.

3. That one ultimate end of life is the same both here, before death, and in heaven after death. Earth is preparation for heaven. If we do not learn to practice the end for which we were made now, we will not be able to do it eternally.

4. That end is sanctity. Charles Peguy wrote these true and profound words: "There is only one tragedy: not to have been a saint."

5. Sanctity means love. To be a saint is nothing more or less than to love God with your whole heart, soul, mind, and strength, and your neighbor as yourself.

6. This love is a matter of will, not feelings. It is a free choice.

7. The form this love-choice always takes is first of all to say yes to God with your whole heart-will-center-self-I-person. This was Mary's secret of sanctity: one word: "*Fiat* (be it done)" to God's angel.

8. Every minute of every day, in everything we do, we can and should enact this conformity to God's will. "Whether you eat or drink or whatever you do, do all to the glory of God."

9. Why don't we do this? Sin. We are sinners. Sin means putting yourself before God. That is the essence of all sin: selfishness. That was the first sin, both of man and of Satan. An angel cannot be tempted to lust or greed or cowardice, but even an angel can be tempted to "me first." And so can we.

   Just as "thy will be done" is the good in every good, "*my* will be done" is the evil in every evil.

10. If you want to be a saint, God will make you one, in his (short or long) time. An old Southern Baptist preacher put it this way (the theology is not quite accurate, but the point is): "God votes for you and the devil votes against you and you cast the deciding vote."

    The old English writer William Law put it something like this—if you will consider your own self, calmly and at leisure, for but one moment in complete honesty, you must come to the admission that there is one and only one reason why you are not, even now, a saint: you do not wholly want to be.

    To want to be a saint, but not *wholly* to want to be a saint—that is the position most of us Christians are in now.

    For as soon as we wholly want to be saints, we *are* saints! Being a saint is not a matter of attaining something previously willed, so that there can be any gap between the willing and the attaining. Being a saint is wholly a matter of willing.

11. Therefore, a practical suggestion: If you do not love God with your whole heart, but you *desire* with your whole heart to love God with your whole heart, then pray continually to God to give you a clean heart (Ps 51:10), an undivided heart, a pure heart. (For "Purity of Heart Is to Will One Thing," to quote Kierkegaard's title.)

    This pure heart is a grace. We cannot produce it ourselves, no matter how hard we try. It comes to us as a gift from God alone. What we can do is to want it with our whole heart and to pray for it.

12. Will God answer that prayer? It is absolutely certain that he will. Why is this absolutely certain? Because he promised exactly that: "Blessed are those who hunger and thirst after righteousness [sanctity], for they shall be filled" (Mt 5:6).

Few things in life are absolute certainties. The solemn promises of God incarnate are absolute certainties.

P.S. I also personally assure you that all the progress in this direction toward this end, however infinitesimally tiny, that I have ever made in fifty-seven years of living, has come about precisely through becoming like a child: more simple, not more complex; and that even a tiny progress down this road is far and away the most ecstatically joyful and the most peacefully satisfying experience this world has to offer.

FOUR

Lesson One in Prayer

Let's get very, very basic and very, very practical about prayer.

The single most important piece of advice I know about prayer is also the simplest: *Just do it!*

How to do it is less important than just doing it. Less-than-perfect prayer is infinitely better than no prayer; more perfect prayer is only finitely better than less perfect prayer.

Nancy Reagan was criticized for her simple anti-drug slogan: "Just say no." But there was wisdom there: the wisdom that the heart of any successful program to stop anything must be the simple will to say no. ("Just say no" doesn't mean that nothing else was needed, but that without that simple decision nothing else would work. "Just say no" may not be ***sufficient*** but it is ***necessary***.)

Similarly, no program, method, book, teacher, or technique will ever succeed in getting us to ***start*** doing anything unless there is first of all that simple, absolute choice to do it. "Just say yes."

The major obstacle in most of our lives to just saying yes to prayer, the most popular and powerful excuse we give for not praying, or not praying more, or not praying regularly, is that we have no time.

The only effective answer to that excuse, I find, is a kind of murder. You have to kill something, you have to say no to something else, in order to make time to pray. Of course, you will never ***find*** time to pray, you have to ***make*** time to pray. And that means unmaking something else. The only way to install the tenant of prayer in the apartment building of your life is to evict some other tenant from those premises that prayer will occupy. Few of us have any empty rooms available.

Deciding to do that is the first thing. And you probably won't decide to do it, only ***wish*** to do it, unless you see prayer for what it is: a matter of life or death, your lifeline to God, to life itself.

Is this exaggerated? Are there more important things? Love, for instance? We need love absolutely. But the love we need is ***agape,*** the love that only God has and is; so unless we go to God for it, we won't get it. And going to God for it means prayer. So ***unless we pray, we will not love.***

Having got that clear and having made prayer your number one priority, having made a definite decision to do it, we must next rearrange our lives around it. Rearranging your time, preparing time to pray, is like preparing your house to paint. As everyone knows who has done any painting, preparation is three-quarters the work, three-quarters the hassle, and three-quarters the time. The actual painting is a breeze compared with the preparation. The same is true of prayer: the hardest step is preparing a place, a time, a sacred and inviolable part of each day for it.

Prayer is like Thanksgiving dinner. It takes one hour to eat it and ten hours to prepare it. Prayer is like Christmas Day: it took a month of preparation, decoration, and shopping to arrange for that one day. Best of all, prayer is like love. Foreplay is, or should be, most of it. For two people truly and totally in love, all of their lives together is foreplay. Well, prayer is like spiritual love-making. God has waited patiently for you for a long, long time. He longs for you to touch the fringe of his being in prayer, as the woman touched the hem of Christ's garment, so that you can be healed. How many hours did that woman have to prepare for that one-minute touch?

The first and most important piece of practical preparation is scheduling. You absolutely must schedule a regular time for prayer, whether you are a "scheduler" with other things in your life or not. "Catch as catch can" simply won't work for prayer; it will mean less and less prayer, or none at all. One quick minute in the morning to offer your day to God is better than nothing at all, of course, but it is as radically inadequate as one quick minute a day with your wife or husband. You simply must decide each day to free up your schedule so you can pray.

How long a time? That varies with individuals and situations, of course; but the very barest minimum should certainly be at least fifteen minutes. You can't really count on getting much deep stuff going on in less time than that. If fifteen minutes seems too much to you, that fact is powerful proof that you need to pray much more to get your head on straight.

After it becomes more habitual and easy, expand it, double it. And later, double it again. Aim at an hour each day, if you want radical results. (*Do* you? Or are you only playing?)

What time of day is best? The most popular time—bedtime—is usually the worst possible time, for two reasons. First, it tends not to be prime time but garbage time, when you're the least alert and awake. Do you really want to put God in the worst apartment in your building? Should you offer him the sickest sheep in your flock?

Second, it won't work. If you wait until every other obligation is taken care of first before you pray, you simply won't pray. For life today is so cruelly complicated for most of us that "every other obligation" is ***never*** taken care of. Remember, you are going to have to kill other things in order to pray. No way out of that.

The most obvious and usually best time is early in the morning. If you can't delay the other things you do, you simply must get up that much earlier.

Should it be the very first thing? That depends. Some people are alert as soon as they get up; others need to shower and dress to wake up. The important thing is to give God the best time and "just do it."

Place is almost as important as time. You should make one special place where you can be undisturbed. "Catch as catch can" won't work for place either.

What place? Some people are not very sensitive to environment and can even use a bathroom. Others naturally seek beauty: a porch, yard, garden, or walk. (I find praying while taking a walk a good combination of spiritual and physical exercise.)

You probably noticed I haven't said a word about techniques yet. That's because three-quarters is preparation, remember? But what about methods?

I can only speak from my own experience as a continuing beginner. The two most effective methods I have found are very simple. One is praying Scripture, reading and praying at the same time, reading in God's presence, receiving the words from God's mouth. The second is spontaneous verbal prayer. I am not good at all at silent prayer, mental prayer, contemplative prayer; my thoughts hop around like fleas. Praying aloud (or singing) keeps me praying, at least. And I find it often naturally leads to silent prayer, or "mental prayer," or contemplation.

Most advice on prayer focuses on higher levels: contemplative prayer. But I suspect many of my readers are prayer infants too, and need to learn to walk before they can run. So these are some lessons from one man's prayer kindergarten. Let's "just do it" even if "it" is only crawling towards God.

P.S. One other practical point: The rosary is the perfect

prayer for scatterbrains. You can also do it on the run—driving, or waiting in line. I pray for ten people, one Hail Mary each, for each of the mysteries, holding up each person into the mystery for Mother's blessing.

The rosary is "mechanical," or automatic. So are most of the dark messages we get from our culture. We need an antidote, a gentle, almost unconscious, reminder of the kingdom. What harm to put Hail Mary ruts in our minds' fields?

PART TWO

Sanctity

FIVE

Seven Steps to Heaven

There are only two kinds of people in the world: those who think there are only two kinds of people in the world and those who don't.

Modern Americans have a deep prejudice against classifying people. The strongest conviction of most of my Catholic college students is that all persons are created equal. More, that they are still equal: sinner and saint, Madonna and *the* Madonna. The latest extension of equality is now to animals.

God's Word is very un-American; it classifies us into two radically distinct groups: the heaven-bound and the hell-bound, the twice-born and the once-born, Christ's progeny and Adam's.

The saints and mystics have added to this twofold classification a further subdivision of steps on the heaven-bound path, degrees of ascent, rungs on Jacob's ladder.

It is not my intention to further complicate these classifications but to simplify them, to suggest seven simple steps to heaven, seven stages of life's journey from Adam to Christ, from sin to salvation. Its purpose is to chart our progress, so we can see how far we need to go and how far we've come, to look behind to avoid sliding back, and to look ahead to "press on to the mark of the high calling of God" (Phil 3:14).

There are seven stages, and thus seven kinds of people. We have all met them. We can call them the nasty, the nice, the good, the converted, the consecrated, the sanctified, and the saints. The six conversions that take us from lower to higher stages are social, moral, mental, personal, volitional, and total conversion.

1. First, we have people whose fundamental philosophy of life is "me first," and they show this. They are obviously selfish: nasty, unkind, unhelpful. They need not be sociopaths or drug dealers. The reason they hurt others may be that they have been hurt themselves, and they became largely extensions of their victimizers. Our seven-step scale is not a hierarchy of blame, but of behavior.

2. Secondly, there are the "nice" people, who are pleasant to be with, but who follow the identical philosophy of "me first." But they have learned some social moves to pacify, amuse, or please others. They are *socially* converted. They are often called delightful people, yet they are at heart selfish.

3. Unselfishness begins when we try to avoid harming others. In stage three, the beginning of ***moral*** conversion, we still "look out for number one," but check in with others first to be sure we're not hurting them by this selfishness that still remains closest to our heart.

4. Minimally religious people also check in with God, so to speak, as well as with others. They try to avoid sin. But what is deepest in their hearts is still their own pleasure and advantage, their own will and way. They just make two com-

promises—with others and with God. (Those in group three make one—with others only.) For instance, they parcel out to God a little of *their* time and money.

5. In stage five, a radical *personal* conversion, or consecration, has begun. Here we want to escape the egotism which was central to all four previous stages. But we do not yet succeed. Romans 7 describes this stage: "The good that I would, I do not; the evil that I would not, that I do" (v. 15). Here we have one foot in the boat and one on the dock; one will in God and one in ourselves. But we identify with the divine will. For the first time, we would love to give up our own will. But we don't.

6. In stage six, sanctification, we do not merely wish that God's will be the master and rudder and anchor and engine of the soul, but God has now been allowed to come in and displace the self as master, piece by piece. The old self still gives trouble, but only as a rebellious servant, not as the master: "It is no longer I who do it, but sin that dwells in me" (Rom 7:17).

7. Stage seven is the goal: God's will only. "You have died, and your life is hid with Christ in God" (Col 3:3). "I live, nevertheless not I, but Christ lives in me" (Gal 2:20).

All of us must reach step seven, if not in this life, then in the next, via purgatory. Stage seven is heavenly life.

Each step up is a plateau of progress. In the Middle Ages, the books assumed at least step four and told us how to go to step seven. Today, we can assume nothing and must start with step two.

The low state of modern expectations is dramatically illustrated by the fact that the most popular moral philosopher among most Catholic religious and moral educators today is not Augustine or Aquinas, or even Plato or Aristotle, but Lawrence Kohlberg, the Harvard agnostic who committed suicide. Yet his highest (sixth) stage of moral development is equivalent to what was the ***minimal*** stage of morality not only for medieval Christians but also for good Greek pagans like Plato and Aristotle and Romans like Cicero. That stage amounts to the "natural law," doing good things because they are objectively good and right in themselves rather than for any personal advantage.

Most readers of this book are probably at stage five. If so, it can be heartening to see how far you have already come, frightening to see how far back you can fall, and also useful in mapping out the last two steps of the way we all must and will walk to come to God's heaven.

There is one and only one possible road to joy: selfless love. These are the seven steps along it.

SIX

Is Sanctity Impractical?

Machiavelli says it is: "The ideals of the ancients are like the stars: very beautiful, but too high and remote to cast light on the dark and perilous roads of this world." He prefers a lantern to a star: a lower ideal, a lesser light.

Jesus says the opposite.

Are we sure we are with Jesus on this one, and not with Machiavelli? Isn't one of the devil's most successful lies the idea that sanctity is impractical, ethereal, otherworldly, something for monks and mystics but not housewives or businessmen or teenagers?

"I can't be a saint; I'm too busy with my business."

Your primary employer is God. Your primary business is God's business. To put yours before his is, strictly speaking, robbery.

"I can't be a saint; I have kids. Having fits is more reasonable than having kids today. If you don't know that, come out of your monastery for a while."

Being a saint is the *only* way you can raise kids today here in Sodom and Gomorrah without losing your sanity or your kids' souls.

"I can't be a saint; I'm a lawyer."

Good joke, but you forgot St. Thomas More. If he can do it, you can do it.

Business or busyness does not make sanctity impossible. It's not even an *obstacle* to sanctity. It's the *precondition* for sanctity.

We could never become saints under the best conditions, only under the worst conditions. Suppose we could create the best conditions. Suppose we could design our own world around ourselves. In that world there would be only happy and fulfilling work, plenty of leisure time, Caribbean surroundings, no creditors, car crashes, crimes, or cancers.

We could no more become saints under such conditions than a lump of marble could become a great sculpture without being touched by the chisel.

The daily frets and obligations and impositions on our will and time are precisely what sanctity is made of. They are its matter; our attitudes and choices are the form.

The world is a giant sculptor's shop. Most of us are familiar with the idea that we need to suffer the strokes of God's chisel to become saints. But we often forget that busyness is a form of suffering.

In fact, I think God finds direct physical pain a less effective form of "chiseling" than impositions on our time, freedom, and power. We have more choice in how we react and use these hassles than we usually do with pain.

The most prosaic place in the world has golden doors to heaven in it, if we would have eyes to see. The diaper-changing table can be made into a clandestine rendezvous with our divine lover, if only we answer his coded invitation.

This is not daydreaming. This is waking up. This is practical. It's *worldliness* that daydreams the devil's dream of happiness on earth, the dream we fell into in Eden, the dream Jesus' alarm bell tries to wake us out of.

No one who ever walked on our planet ever uttered a more practical sentence than this one: "What does it profit a man if he gain the whole world and lose his own soul?"

The most impractical, unprofitable business deal you can make is to sell your soul for anything or everything in this world.

Nothing is more solidly certain than the fact that we will die. Nothing is more obvious than that this life in time is a tiny thing, a pea, a mustard seed, compared to eternity. Nothing is more practical than to plant that seed here for an eternal harvest, to invest your lifetime in God's Bank of Eternity that offers infinite interest.

This world is full of dreamers, all dreaming different varieties of the same dream, the magic spell we let the devil cast over us in Eden. I call it the "if only" dream. "If only I had a million dollars, or if only I could get away from this problem or these people or this place, if only I could go back and do it over again, do it differently... then I would be happy."

This dream has never worked, never come true. Not once. Yet they keep believing the "if only" dream. And they call *that* practical and realistic, and call sanctity "impractical" and "unrealistic." That's like Scrooge calling Santa stingy.

Pascal puts it simply. Here are the two most obvious facts about human life and the obvious conclusion to be drawn from them:

1. "All men seek happiness. There are no exceptions."
2. "Yet for very many years no one without faith has ever reached the goal at which everyone is continually aiming. All men complain: princes, subjects, nobles, commoners, old, young, strong, weak, learned, ignorant, healthy, sick, in every country, at every time, of all ages and all conditions."
3. (Conclusion) "A test which has gone on so long, without pause or change, really ought to convince us that we are incapable of attaining happiness by our own efforts."

Worldliness is for dreamers; sanctity is for realists. Materialistic hopes for happiness are pure blind faith; only saints are happy.

We will never be happy in this world until we stop treating it as our home and start treating it as our gymnasium. It's a terrible home, but a great gym. And there are opportunities in it every minute for every one of us to attain happiness by the only tried-and-true road ever found, the only practical philosophy of life ever discovered: sanctity. Its secret of joy is simply to spell correctly: *J*esus first, *O*thers second, *Y*ourself third.

SEVEN

The Relevance of Saints

Be honest: Isn't there something in you that thinks of a saint as an Everest that you cannot climb? Even if your theological wisdom knows better, isn't there another voice, based on your experience, that tells you that you really know better? That saints are fine as heroes but hardly as models for us struggling, straggling schnooks and schlemiels—isn't that true? We are soft and spoiled, and they are too hard, too fanatical for us to relate to them—or else our hearts are too hard and encased, and theirs are too soft, too infinitely loving, for us to relate to them—isn't that true?

No, it isn't. It is precisely when we are the most confused, unwise, tepid, tempted, weak, and lost that the saints are the most practically useful to us. Our Father in heaven and our Holy Mother Church would never have given them to us if this were not so. And you know that, deep down.

There are at least two ways the saints are immediately, practically relevant to us. First, they prove to us that the life of sanctity *can* be lived, that anyone can climb this Everest just as they did. For they were all exactly like us. Not one of them came out of his mother's womb wearing a halo. Secondly, they show us not only *that* it can be done but also *how*, in detail. They are empirical data, accessible to all, just as in science.

Briefly, I want to explore this second way the saints are relevant to us, this *how*-to-do-it relevance. It is an answer to the question of "discernment"—a very practical question if ever there was one. Let me try to explain the connection.

The problem of discernment can be stated very simply: How do we know God's will for us? In general, we know because he has told us, in his Word and through his church. But how do we find out what he has not publicly told us there? He has revealed general principles for all, but not practical applications to each individual life. We want to apply these principles as he wills, but how do we find out how he wills?

Let me give three examples.

1. During the last few months, I heard one sermon recommending "assertiveness training" and another warning against it. Both priests were trying to help us to follow God's will for our lives. How are we to know which to believe?

2. During the last few years, I have read a number of books by serious Catholics advocating the use of "centering prayer" as a powerful device for knowing and loving God. I have also read books by serious Catholics warning against this technique as not Christian and leading away from the true God.

3. During the last thirty years or so the church has been tragically split between those who emphasize social justice and charity and positive good deeds and attack the "old hang-ups on sin" as unhealthy; and those who emphasize individual and private holiness, prayer, sacrifice, and character-building (especially overcoming our favorite sins—lust and greed) as

the heart of holiness and prior to public good works. How do we know which emphasis is closest to God's heart and will for us?

Scripture does not address these problems explicitly, for they are explicitly contemporary problems. The church has not officially pronounced a specific solution to them, as she has to such issues as contraception, abortion, and divorce (all no), or capitalism, cremation, and evolution (all a qualified yes). Catholics who seek guidance from Scripture and the church have come to opposite conclusions on these and other issues. How do we discern what God's will is in such confusion?

The answer to the problem of discernment is simple in theory. It is found in John 7:17. When Jesus was asked this question, "How can we understand your teaching?", he replied: "If your will were to do the will of my Father, you would understand my teaching." The secret to discernment is sanctity. The secret to knowing God's will is willing God's will.

The problem, though, is that we are not very good at that. It looks like a Catch-22: We need discernment to become saints, but we need to be saintly to discern. And we are far from that, far from perfectly obeying the first and greatest commandment, to love God with our whole heart and soul. We lack the close experiential familiarity with God that would make discernment easy for us.

This is where the saints help. They are like big brothers and sisters who know the mind of the Father better than we do. When you are unsure, follow the leader. Go by precedent. Imitate those wiser than yourself. Be a conformist in what you're not very good at. Be creative and original and nonconformist only in what you are very good at. Now most of us are not very good at sanctity, so we should be conformists there, we should follow in the footsteps of those who have followed in the footsteps of Christ. We should follow our betters. (Of course the saints are our betters; if they are not, why should we imitate them?)

The saints are ***data.*** They make discernment almost scientific. For we can investigate this data—their lives and writings—empirically. How did they solve the problems we are wrestling with, or similar problems? What did they write that addresses our problems? There is an immense body of riches here, and not to be acquainted with it is inexcusable. Not to have taught the lives of the saints is even more inexcusable for Catholic educators, and merits the millstone-of-the-month award (Mt 18:6).

The saints are little Christs. They are stained glass windows of variegated colors, through whom the one pure white light of Christ shines in all the colors of the human spectrum, into all the corners of the church, just as the windows of a great cathedral do.

For instance, the saints solve the three discernment problems mentioned above.

1. They are assertive, not wimpy. St. Catherine even corrected the pope when he wimped out, just as St. Paul had done (Gal 2:11). It is not for their own rights or expression of their "personality" that the saints assert themselves, but for *the* right, for God's rights, for Truth. They are assertive, but they do not assert *themselves* anymore than they suppress themselves. They *deny* themselves, that is, their selfish wills, and *forget* themselves, and keep their eyes and their hearts on God. They do not have ingrown eyeballs; they are not spiritually self-caressing auto-erotics. Nor are they smarmy, unctuous, self-resenting neurotics. The typical expression of sanctity is martyrdom. Martyrs are certainly assertive, not wimpy; but they are not assertive in the same way and for the same reason as secular psychology teaches.

2. The saints are all for prayer, of course, and in it they touch their center, the eye of the hurricane, the place of peace. They value (and practice) silence and contemplation far more than we do. We think our parishes are spiritually successful if and only if they are hives of busy bee-ing. We are

activists, Marthas; the saints are all Marys first, then some (but not all) are activists. But their "centering prayer" centers not on themselves, or on nothing, but on Christ. And it is a centering of will and love, not just mind and consciousness. So it is like modern "centering prayer" in some ways, and unlike it in others. So why borrow techniques from Oriental religions when you have in your own backyard ones that have worked and ones you know are God-approved?

3. Finally, all the saints see both public good works ***and*** private prayer and self-discipline as absolutely necessary. Sanctity to them is not a supermarket. They eat everything on their plate. They fight as hard against personal sin as any conservative and as hard against public injustice as any liberal.

The saints are our big brothers and sisters. We are to grow into them. We ***will*** grow into their shoes, if not in this life then in the next, through purgatorial re-education. For God is no compromiser. Like any good father, he is "easy to please but hard to satisfy," said the Scottish writer George MacDonald. He will keep us at it until we get our lessons right. Saints are not freaks, but models. They are our job description. Nothing could be more relevant and practical.

EIGHT

Joy

Joy is more than happiness, just as happiness is more than pleasure. Pleasure is in the body. Happiness is in the mind and feelings. Joy is deep in the heart, the spirit, the center of self.

The way to pleasure is power and prudence. The way to happiness is moral goodness. The way to joy is sanctity, loving God with your whole heart and your neighbor as yourself.

Everyone wants pleasure. More deeply, everyone wants happiness. Most deeply, everyone wants joy.

Freud says that spiritual joy is a substitute for physical pleasure. People become saints out of sexual frustrations.

This is exactly the opposite of the truth. St. Thomas Aquinas says, "No man can live without joy. That is why one deprived of spiritual joy goes over to carnal pleasures." Sanctity is never a substitute for sex, but sex is often a substitute for sanctity.

The simplest, most unanswerable proof that Aquinas is right and Freud is wrong, is experience. It is not a matter of faith alone. It has been proved by experience by many, many people, many, many times. You can repeat the experiment and prove it to yourself. You can be absolutely certain that it is true, just as you can be certain that fire is hot and ice is cold.

Millions of people for thousands of years have tried the experiment and not one of them has ever been cheated. All who seek, find—this is not just a promise about the next life, to be believed by faith, but a promise about this life, to be proved by experience, to be tested by experiment.

No one who ever said to God, "Thy will be done" and meant it with his heart, ever failed to find joy—not just in heaven, or even down the road in the future in this world, but in this world at that very moment, here and now.

In the very act of self-surrender to God there is joy. Not just later, as a consequence, but right then. It is exactly like a woman's voluntary sexual surrender to a man. The mystics often say all souls are female to God; that's one reason why God is always symbolized as male. Of course it's only a symbol, but it's a true symbol, a symbol of something true.

The symbolism is not "sexist" either. It holds for a man's soul as well. Only when lovers give up all control and melt helplessly into each other's bodies and spirits, only when they overcome the fear that demands control, do they find the deepest joy. Frigidity, whether sexual or spiritual, comes from egotism.

We've all known people who are cold, suspicious, mistrusting, unable to let go. These people are miserable, wretched. They can't find joy because they can't trust, they can't have faith. You need faith to love, and you need to love to find joy. Faith, love, and joy are a package deal.

Every time I have ever said yes to God with something even slightly approaching the whole of my soul, every time I have not only ***said*** "Thy will be done" but meant it, loved it, longed for it—I have never failed to find joy and peace ***at that moment.*** In fact, to the precise extent that I have said it and meant it, to exactly that extent, have I found joy.

Every other Christian who has ever lived has found exactly the same thing in his own experience. It is an experiment that has been performed over and over again billions of times, always with the same result. It is as certain as gravity.

It sounds too good to be true. It sounds like pious exaggeration, a salesman's pitch. Instant joy? All you have to do is surrender to God? What's the catch?

There *is* a catch. It's a big one, but a simple one: you have to really do it, not just think about it.

To do it completely requires something we dislike very much: death. Not the death of the body. The body is not the obstacle. The ego is. Self-will is. We fear giving *that* up even more than we fear giving up our body to death—even though that ego, the thing St. Paul calls "the old man" in us, or the Adam in us, is the cause of all our misery.

That old self has sold itself to the devil. It's his microphone. It sits there behind our ears chattering away. When we're about to give ourselves to God, it instantly whispers to us: "Careful, now. Hold back. Don't get too close to him. He's dangerous. In fact, he's a killer."

The voice speaks some truth. Even the devil has to begin with some truth in order to twist it into a lie. It's true; God is a killer. If you let him, he will kill your old, selfish, unhappy, bored, wretched, mistrusting, loveless self.

But he will do it only if you want him to; and he will do it only as much as you want him to. God is a gentleman. He will never rape your soul, only woo it.

And when he does, you'll understand one of the reasons why sex is so different, so special, so holy: it is an image of *this*, of heaven, of the ultimate meaning and destiny and purpose of your life.

Even the tiny foretaste of heaven that we can all have here on earth by surrendering to God is much more joyful than the greatest ecstasy sex can give, just as being with your beloved is more joyful than being with her picture.

You either believe all this, or you don't. If you do, then do it! If you don't, then try it. You'll like it.

NINE

Learning Something from Zen

The documents of Vatican II say Christians can learn things from other religions without compromising or demeaning their own. I would like to try to do that now, and learn something useful, something Christianly useful, from Zen Buddhism, which is the non-Christian religion I happen to know the most about.

To learn this, we need not believe Buddhism is true. Nor do we need to believe it is false. It is not a question of truth, or theology, that I want to explore here. I only want to *use* two features in Zen Buddhism to highlight and appreciate two parallel features in Christianity that we usually take for granted; two features which, if we only treated them as passionately as Zen Buddhists treat the two parallel features in their religion, would transform our lives and our happiness.

First, in Zen, as in any form of Buddhism, "enlightenment" (*satori)* is everything. It is total joy (Buddha called it "bliss"), the ultimate end and point and purpose of existence, the meaning of life. It is more important than life itself. The disciple treats it as *more* than "a matter of life or death," for he willingly risks or sacrifices his life for it. He performs the most arduous and bizarre tasks in the hope that they will lead to it, for it is quite reasonable to invest even a great good in order to win an even greater one, a "pearl of great price" (Mt 13:46).

The second feature is that the *roshi* or spiritual director must be totally trusted. He has attained enlightenment, and he knows the way to it. The way is long, hard, and usually surprising, even shocking. The *roshi* commands the disciple to do things like sitting fourteen hours a day in a painful posture staring at a wall, or struggling with an unsolvable puzzle (a *koan*) night and day for a lifetime, or doing nothing but sweeping the floor for twenty years. The disciple does all these things only because he trusts the *roshi*, not himself. That is why Zen is a religion. All the religions of the world have this one feature in common: they are based on some kind of trust.

Now let us look at the parallels to these two things in our own religion.

First, our enlightenment is heaven, the beatific vision, union with God, our sharing in the very life and love and mind of God. It is bliss, infinite joy, because God is infinite joy. Even if everything the Buddhist says about Buddhist enlightenment is true, our goal is more than the Buddhist goal, not less. It includes everything in it and goes beyond it.

Second, we have a *roshi* too, one who is infinitely wiser and more trustable than any human *roshi*. Our *roshi* is Jesus Christ, God incarnate. He is with us now instructing us, for he has promised, "Lo, I am with you all days, even to the end of the world" (Mt 28:20). His Father holds the reins of all the horses that run on our life's race track. His Spirit literally lives in us, possesses us, haunts us. Nothing escapes his providential plan for our life—not the fall of a sparrow, not a hair on our head.

The Buddhist *roshi* works with his disciple only a few hours a day, and usually in groups. Our *roshi* works with us every second of every day, and works individually, tailoring every event he allows to come into our lives to the end of our individual need, and he does his tailoring with infinite care, wisdom, love, and control. That is why "*all* things work together for good for those who love God, those who are called according to his purpose" (Rom 8:28). There is not a thing in our lives—not a cancer, not a candy, not a war, not a wart—that is not there precisely because our almighty, all-loving, and all-wise *roshi* deliberately allowed it as part of our training program, part of his lesson plan, for the one and only purpose of bringing us most effectively to our end, our enlightenment.

If we were good Buddhists, we would expend every ounce of passion and energy and desire and determination toward the end of enlightenment, and also toward the means to that end that our *roshi* gives to us, no matter how painful, protracted, or puzzling those ways and means may be. For we would desire enlightenment infinitely and trust the *roshi* totally.

As Christians we have a similar opportunity—no, invitation—no, privilege—no, obligation—no, *necessity* to do no less to our *roshi*, who is God himself.

What does that mean concretely and practically and in detail? How does it transform our lives? It means that when we have to perform or endure some meaningless or trivial or frustrating task like waiting in some long bureaucratic line, or picking up after the kids for the millionth time, we must do these things actively and passionately, not passively—as disciples eagerly performing the tasks perfectly designed by the wise *roshi*, learning our special lessons, playing our special music, practicing our special parts in the play, treading our special highway to heaven.

We can totally trust our *roshi* even when he seems to have gone crazy or asleep, because human *roshis* sometimes go crazy or asleep, but the divine *roshi* never does.

If all this is not true, then either there is no God at all, or he is not present in our lives, or he is weak and does not have the whole world in his hands, or he is bad or indifferent and does not love us and care for us, or he is stupid and makes mistakes in guiding us. These are the five essential heresies of atheism, deism, paganism, pantheism, and naturalism. To embrace any one of these is to fundamentally abandon the faith. There is no comfortable compromise, no middle path. Either we must deny God's existence, presence, power, love, or wisdom; or else we must deny ourselves and our own natural tendency to look at this "accident" or that "loss" or that "tragedy" as a mistake on the part of our *roshi*. Either God is our perfect *roshi* and everything is from his light and toward our enlightenment, or else we have no reliable *roshi* at all and we are adrift in the darkness.

Look at the pen or the needle or the shovel or the wheel in your hand now as the gift given to you straight from the hand and heart and mind of God—because it *is*.

TEN

How the Sea Can Help You Pray

Everyone living today in America in or near a city has a desperate need for the three S's: silence, solitude, and slowing down—for both psychological sanity and prayer.

1. *Silence.* Kierkegaard, the great nineteenth century Danish Christian philosopher, spoke often of silence. Almost the last thing he ever wrote about was silence. He said: "If I were a physician, and if I were allowed to prescribe just one remedy for all the ills of the modern world, I would prescribe silence. For even if the Word of God were proclaimed in the modern world, how could one hear it with so much noise? Therefore, *create silence.*"

   Silence is necessary; it is not a luxury. Only words that come from silence carry power; words that come from noise, or only from other words, are shallow. Words from silence are like waves from the ocean; words from other words are like babbling brooks at best, at worst like emptying faucets and drains and toilets.

2. *Solitude.* Solitude is something any ancient sage would long foı as a gift. Yet it is the very thing our society has imposed on its most desperate criminals as the cruellest torture it can contrive.

   Solitude too, is a necessity, not a luxury; for it is the necessary basis of true community. Community without solitude is like a hundred people in a circle each leaning on the next one. Soon the whole circle tips over.

3. *Slowing down.* Slowing down has become almost impossible today. Life is like a mad white-water river, and boats are capsizing right and left. What we need is to be led beside still waters, so that our souls can be refreshed.

   Slowing down is also necessary, for it is the source of all effective activity—like the deeds and words of Christ. Like slowly pulling a bowstring, then suddenly letting it go. The shallow think that only restless souls are alive, but the deep know that only quiet souls are truly alive.

God provided nature for us for many reasons. Three of them are to help us to silence, solitude, and slowing down.

I know from experience that time spent with nature can be an investment in the Bank of Heaven. For there is a wonderful and mysterious power in nature to free us from noise, crowds, and rush, and to steep our souls in silence, solitude, and slowing down. I also know from experience that it is difficult to pray, and impossible to pray well, without silence, solitude, and slowing down.

Unfortunately, most of the people today who know this spiritual power of nature are not Christians but New Age flakes, earth-worshipers, or Buddhists. That is probably one reason why Christians are suspicious of this message: because it is being preached by such suspicious messengers. But it is part of the truth, and even non-Christians know it. Nature abhors a vacuum spiritually as well as physically; and in our spiritually-starved secularistic society, if we do not lead people to silence, solitude, and slowing down, someone else will. And it will sell. Even crumbs of it will sell to starving souls.

What *happens* when we just meander with nature for a while

instead of making something happen? What happens when we forget clocks and obligations, and just watch waves, or stars, or clouds, or sunsets, or rivers? In my experience, at least two things almost always happen. One is natural, the other supernatural. The natural effect can be described as an overall feeling of refreshment, like cool water in a desert, or a calm after a battle. The supernatural effect is that I can pray better, and want to pray more.

I think the natural effect helps cause the supernatural effect. It fertilizes the soil. It's like psychoanalysis: it's not religion, but it can remove some of the obstacles to true religion, like addiction, or obsession, or paranoia, or depression. I can't pray well if I'm obsessed, and I can't pray well if I'm noisy inside. I think we are sometimes too quick to pray, too impatient with preliminaries. Every house painter knows you have to spend more time in preparation than in actual painting. And every gardener knows you have to spend more time preparing the garden than seeding it. I suspect the same is true of prayer today.

Perhaps this was not so before the Industrial Revolution. Then, we had a very different relationship with nature and with time. Time was related to the cycles of nature and life—meaningful time, time measured by real events, not by clocks. We must learn to ignore clocks and return to real time. Only then will we escape the slavery of clocks. Clocks are our real Frankenstein's monster. We made them, and now they are stronger than we are.

Here is the most practical way nature aids prayer for me. I find that by far the biggest obstacle to prayer is the excuse that I have no time. But after I spend an hour doing nothing but watching waves on rocks, I find that somehow that excuse has lost all meaning; that time is not something I have, but something I make as I go along like a spider spinning a web.

Different things in nature will do this for different people. For me, it is the sea. Even though I get bored easily, I can very happily sit for an hour and watch the waves. I think there must be something God put into the sea to remind us of himself—an image of infinity and depth and power and mystery and dynamic activity all at once. When I use abstract concepts, even the best ones I can find, they just don't hold it—like an open hand trying to hold the water of a wave. It has to emerge from the experience itself. Like the storm from which God answered Job, it remains a mystery.

But the "bottom line," the "payoff," is that I emerge from my hour with a lesson learned. Nature teaches me *how to listen.* How to listen to waves, and thus how to listen in general, and thus how to listen to God. This is an art I know we all need desperately. If we listened to other people and to God, we would avoid most of our tragedies, wars, divorces, violence, drugs, broken relationships, pains. How can we have faith, hope, and love without listening? How can we enjoy heaven without enjoying listening? How can we be *saved* unless we learn to listen to God?

If nature can help even a few of us even a little way toward that goal, is this not something literally priceless? So try it. What can you lose?

ELEVEN

Surfing and Spirituality

Nothing is more important than our journey to God, or "the spiritual life," as many writers call it. For this is our ultimate reason for living. It's what each of us was born for.

Nearly all who write about the spiritual life distinguish *stages* in it. For it's clearly like a road on which we move, and change, and progress.

Many different images from physical life have been used for the stages of the spiritual life, for example, Teresa of Avila's "mansions" in *The Interior Castle*, or Walter Hilton's rungs on *The Ladder of Perfection*. Since these are just *analogies*, differences between them are not really contradictions. The same reality (the stages in the spiritual life) can be truly told by using many different metaphors, or symbols from physical life.

One analogy that's never, as far as I know, been used—yet one that is quite arresting to many souls—is the analogy of surfing.

Many of us love the ocean. It's our favorite place in the world. As soon as we have the vacation time and money, we spend it there. We feel a mysterious longing for the sea as some kind of secret to our own identity, as if our blood had salt water in it. (It does, by the way.) This longing is a commonplace of poets:

> I must go down to the sea again
> To the lonely sea and the sky
> And all I ask is a tall ship
> And a star to steer her by.
>
> **John Maesfield**

> Roll on, thou deep and dark blue ocean, roll;
> Ten thousand fleets sweep over thee in vain!
>
> **Lord Byron**

We nonpoets feel it too. If we didn't, we wouldn't read and love the poets.

I'm not an expert swimmer, but I ***am*** a swimmer. I'm not a good surfer, not even a "real" surfer with a full-sized board. But surfing with a boogie board, or body-board—well, that *is* my "thing." It's not only one of the most delightful experiences I know but also one of the most profoundly suggestive. I know only a little about the spiritual life, much more from others than from myself. But what I know well (surfing) is a powerful teacher, by analogy, of what I don't know well (the spiritual life). That's the purpose of analogies: to use the better-known to better know the unknown. I here share my favorite analogy because I suspect many readers will reply, "*What!* You too? I thought I was the only one!"

The key elements in the symbolism are pretty clear: I, the surfer, am myself. The body with which I surf in the sea symbolizes the soul, with which I "surf" in God. The sea is God. The beach is the approach to God. Surfing is the experience of God, or the spiritual life.

In my surfing experience, I can distinguish twelve steps. In my experience of God, I can also distinguish twelve steps. The twelve clear, physical steps in surfing help clarify the twelve more mysterious steps in the journey into God.

There are four main divisions, with three subdivisions in each.

The first three steps are preliminaries. The first step is the ***knowledge*** of the sea. No one will ever experience the sea without ***going*** there, and no one will go there without ***wanting*** to, and no one will want to without ***knowing about it***. Thus, the first three steps are: (1) knowing about the sea; (2) wanting to go there; and (3) going there.

Parallel to these three necessary preliminaries for surfing are the three necessary preliminaries to God. They are the three "theological virtues" of faith, hope, and love.

First, we must know that God exists, and is good, and is our joy. That knowledge comes by faith. (It can also come by reason for some, but it comes by faith for all.)

Second, we must hope for God and seek him. "Seek and you shall find" implies that if you don't seek, you won't find.

Third, love (charity, ***agape***) is the fruit of this plant of hope, whose roots are faith. For Christians, love means a life, not a feeling. As Kierkegaard puts it, love is "the works of love." Faith blossoms into works. Faith works. The plant—roots, stem and fruit—is one. Faith, hope, and love-works are not three things but three parts of one living thing: the spiritual life, the life of God in the soul. This is "the one thing needful" (Lk 10:42).

Faith in God is our knowledge of God. This is like our knowledge of the sea. Hope in God is our desire for God. This is like our desire to go to the sea. Love of God is our actual movement and growth toward God, or in God. This is like our actual travel to the sea.

All three are delightful. Planning a vacation is almost half the fun. Foreplay is as much a part of love as consummation.

Our knowledge of the sea need not be deep, like the sea, for it to be sufficient as the first step in our journey. We needn't be oceanographers to be vacationers. Similarly, we needn't be theologians to be saints.

But our *desire* for the sea must be deep if we are to take the time and money to travel there. Mild curiosity isn't enough. Most of us have to move a lot of schedules, people, and suitcases to take a vacation. We won't do it without longing.

The next three stages in our journey to the sea happen only when we are already there, in its "presence": (4) seeing the sea; (5) smelling the sea; and (6) running down the beach into the sea.

The gift of understanding is like sight. No amount of words or verbal explanations can substitute for seeing. You only *believe* the truth of the words in a travel folder. But you *see* the sea when you arrive there, and that sight strikes a chord in the heart, a chord of joy and homecoming—and at the same time of further longing. It's a mysterious mingling of deep satisfaction and dissatisfaction, a divine discontent. For the restless heart that God has made for himself is not only restless until it *gets* to God; it's restless until it rests *in* God.

The faith-hope-love pattern is repeated here. Seeing the sea is the fulfillment of the faith-from-afar that we had from travel folders. And seeing God is the fulfillment of faith: "If you believe, you will see" (Jn 11:40). Smelling the sea is the fulfillment of desiring hope from afar. Smelling is a most mystical sense. The thing itself enters into us, or we into it, when its very molecules enter our noses. And smells move us more deeply and mysteriously, sometimes, than any other sense. Finally, running into the sea is like self-forgetful, self-offering love. It's an obligation, an offering of self.

The next three stages deepen our relationship with the sea and with God. First (7), we get our toes wet. Spiritually, we experience a little of what we have first believed and then understood.

Second (8), we get wet halfway up. Getting your bathing suit wet is the essential step. Bathing suits cover our private parts, our tenderest spots. This symbolizes the hopeful investment of our lives that represent pain, sacrifice, and death. The starkest difference between the saints and ourselves is their willingness, even eagerness, to suffer for God.

Finally (9), getting wet all over symbolizes the total consecration of our whole self, whole will, and whole life to God, leaving absolutely nothing for ourselves, not a penny or a second or any other thing we call our own.

The last three stages cover what is usually called "mystical experience." Getting in over your head (10), with your feet no longer on the ground, symbolizes the mind plunging into the divine mysteries, the "dark night of the soul" that no words can mediate. We lose all footing. We are no longer in control. We're a part of the sea, it seems. Thus, even the orthodox mystics say pantheistic-sounding things, for they see and feel only God, not themselves at all. Of course, they're still *there*—who's having the mystical experience, anyway? But they don't know or feel themselves there anymore. They're in over their heads. This sounds scary only as heaven sounds scary. For it *is* heaven, the beginning or foretaste of heaven. All of us will be mystics there.

Then comes the actual surfing (11). Let's make it body surfing. Body surfing is an even more intimate oneness with the sea than board surfing, whether with a full-sized board or small body-board. Here, our unity with the sea is greater than the passive getting in over your head (10); it is the active doing what the sea does. What the sea does is waving. So we wave. We become one with what the sea *does* as well as one with what the sea *is*.

Steps 1-9 were all dynamic process, motion. Step ten was the end, peace. But that's *not* the end. On the other side of the end there is more dynamism and movement, but this time *from* the end rather than *to* it, from within it, as waves come from within the sea. After we are moved *to* God, we find that once we are in God we are moved again, this time *from* God, *by* God. God is dynamic, like crashing surf, not static, like a stagnant pool. Living in God forever is the most dynamic, exciting thing there is. Body surfing is (for surfing freaks like me) a remote but intimate analogy, a weak yet powerful foretaste of heaven.

Finally, the analogy breaks down, as all do. The last physical stage (12) is not joyful, but the spiritual stage it symbolizes is supreme joy. The last stage is drowning (something I would ***not*** advise!). It symbolizes mystical union, death not just of concepts (stage 10) or of self-will (stage 11, when we're moved wholly by the sea's waves) but of the very ego-self itself. Something in us longs to die, for only death brings resurrection. Something in us that we cannot understand, something we both fear and love, cries out to God to slay us in the Spirit:

> Blow, blow, blow till I be
> But the breath of the Spirit,
> blowing in me.

And, "I live, nevertheless not I, but Christ lives in me."

PART THREE

Our Daily Walk

TWELVE

How to Become a Saint While Changing Diapers

Throughout the history of the church, the needs of each age have brought forth new spiritual disciplines, new forms of spiritual exercises, new roads to sanctity to fit those new needs. When the decadent pagan Roman Empire was collapsing, monks flocked to the Egyptian desert, definitively breaking with the dying world. When Europe needed a bridge over the Dark Ages, a bridge joining the old civilization with the new, monks copied manuscripts. When life became relatively secure in the Middle Ages, mendicant orders of begging friars appeared. When the Black Death and the Protestant Reformation turned individuals inward, more introspective forms of sanctity appeared. When wars of religion devastated Europe, the Jesuits emphasized spiritual warfare.

Today the dominant feature of our lives is technology. We are surrounded by machines, labor-saving devices, time-saving devices. And the result is that we have no time, no leisure. The ways to sanctity that were fit for a simple age are no longer workable. We are all so harried and hassled by obligations, like worried little rabbits hopping around serving our machines, that we have little free time, even for God.

There are only three ways an inner life can fit into this world. (1) We can simply refuse that world, swap cars for bikes, TVs for books, cities for farms. Few of us are free to do that even if we want to. (2) We can fit God into the tiny, little, empty places left, develop a McDonald's sanctity, spiritual fast food, one-minute meditations, "quality time" for God—a euphemism for hurried, *non*quality times. Obviously, (1) and (2) are unsatisfactory. The only alternative is (3) to sanctify our busyness, our work. The sanctification of work is perhaps the greatest need of our times from the standpoint of sanctity.

But how? How do we find God in the middle of a busy day? How do we carry God with us from the Eucharist to the office? How do we overcome the separation between prayer and life by making all life a prayer? *Ora et labora* (pray and work) was the Benedictine motto; but today we need to do even more, we need to know how to make work *be* prayer, to make prayer *out of* our daily work.

Five hints, five helps toward an answer, come to my mind. I doubt whether anyone ever put these five together before, for those who are "into" one of them are not usually "into" another. But they are (1) St. Thomas More, (2) Teilhard de Chardin, (3) Opus Dei, (4) Ghandi, and (5) Mother Teresa.

1. St. Thomas More is a model, a hero, a "man for all seasons"—the title of the movie about him which is my candidate for the greatest movie ever made. He did it; busy lawyer, politician, man-of-the-world, yet in and through and because of this "secular" activity he became a saint (and, indeed, a martyr, the crown of sanctity). How did he do it? See the movie.

2. Most of the current disciples of Teilhard de Chardin seem to me to be corn flakes; but Teilhard himself, I think had some very valuable things to say to us in *The Divine Milieu* on the subject of sanctifying daily work. His theological and theoretical works

may be dangerous (the Vatican issued a 'monitum,' or warning, against them) or may not (Cardinal Henri De Lubac, himself both brilliant and orthodox, staunchly defended Teilhard's orthodoxy), but his practical advice I find precious. He introduces an eschatological dimension into our work. Not only our *operatio* but also our *opus*, not only our acts of working but also the works we produce, will somehow be used by God to make up the "new heavens and the new earth." We are to do the very best work we can because that work is to be part of God's eternal kingdom, unimaginably transformed by death and resurrection. We are cooperating with God right now in building this new world; our pen, or shovel, or computer, is the extension of the fingers of Christ, of the body of Christ. I highly recommend the first half of *The Divine Milieu* on this.

3. Opus Dei's whole reason for existence is to address the problem of the sanctification of daily work directly and explicitly. Its fundamental answer is traditional: to *offer up* our work to God, to pour the infinitely precious soul of a pure intention, a God-ward intention, into every secular action. Teilhard's answer confers the hope of resurrection on the bodies of our acts, and Opus Dei's gives immortality to their soul.

4. Ghandi says he learned the secret of spiritual detachment in the midst of committed worldly action from the *bhakti* yoga taught in the *Bhagavad-Gita*. Yes, it's a Hindu book, not a Christian one; but is *everything* in Hinduism wrong? Did not Vatican II encourage us to study and profit from the wisdom in other world religions? Here, it seems to me, is a prime example, a pearl of wisdom. The way to sanctity amidst activity is to work not for the fruit of the work, not out of desire for success, not looking forward, but looking backward, so to speak, to the source and motive of the act: love and duty and obedience to God. Do what you do because it is your God-given task now. If you act out of desire for success, you bind yourself to the fear of failure. If we will only one thing—God's will—we are free.

5. Only a saint can be as simple as Mother Teresa. She has a way of summing up all of life in one sentence. The unforgettable and precious sentence is: "God did not put me here to be successful. God put me here to be faithful."

How liberating! If Martha had only known that, she could have been as saintly as Mary. Contemplation (Mary) is ***not*** superior to action (Martha) unless it carries out God's will. *That* is the "one thing needful." Picking up a pin for the love of God is sanctity. Saving the whole world for any other reason is not.

These are just five seeds. Perhaps some day soon God will raise up a great saint who will teach us how to grow a whole garden from them. Pray for that teacher, and meanwhile use the ones we have.

THIRTEEN

Twelve Ways to Know God

Jesus defines eternal life as knowing God (Jn 17:3). What are the ways? In how many different ways can we know God, and thus know eternal life? When I take an inventory, I find twelve.

1. The final, complete, definitive way, of course, is *Christ*, God himself in human flesh.

2. His *church* is his body, so we know God also through the church.

3. The *Scriptures* are the church's book. This book, like Christ himself, is called "The Word of God."

4. Scripture also says we can know God in *nature*—see Romans 1. This is an innate, spontaneous, natural knowledge. I think no one who lives by the sea, or by a little river, can be an atheist.

5. *Art* also reveals God. I know three ex-atheists who say, "There is the music of Bach, therefore there must be a God." This too is immediate.

6. *Conscience* is the voice of God. It speaks absolutely, with no ifs, ands, or buts. This too is immediate.

The last three ways of knowing God (4-6) are natural, while the first three are supernatural. The last three reveal three attributes of God, the three things the human spirit wants most: truth, beauty, and goodness. God has filled his creation with these three things. Here are six more ways in which we can and do know God.

7. *Reason*, reflecting on nature, art, or conscience, you can know God by good philosophical arguments.

8. *Experience*, life, your story, can also reveal God. You can see the hand of Providence there.

9. The collective experience of the race, embodied in history and tradition, expressed in literature, also reveals God. You can know God through others' stories, through great literature.

10. The *saints* reveal God. They are advertisements, mirrors, little Christs. They are perhaps the most effective of all means of convincing and converting people.

11. Our ordinary daily experience of *doing God's will* will reveal God. God becomes clearer to see when the eye of the heart is purified: "Blessed are the pure of heart, for they shall see God."

12. *Prayer* meets God—ordinary prayer. You learn more of God from a few minutes of prayerful repentance than through a lifetime in a library.

Unfortunately, Christians sometimes have family fights about these ways, and treat them as either/or instead of both/and. They all support each other, and nothing could be more foolish than treating them as rivals—for example, finding God in the church versus finding God in nature, or reason versus experience, or Christ versus art.

If you have neglected any of these ways, it would be an excellent idea to explore them. For instance, pray using great music. Or take an hour to review your life some time to see God's role in your past. Read a great book to better meet and know and glorify God. Pray about it first.

Add to this list, if you can. There are more ways of finding and knowing God than any one essay can contain. Or any one world.

FOURTEEN

Time

Recently I was late getting a manuscript to an editor. My excuse? By far the most popular one in America: I had "no time." Let's examine that excuse. Why do we all seem to have no time for anything, much less for prayer?

I am constantly feeling guilty about this, and I suspect most of you are too. I think the single biggest obstacle to our relationship with God (after sin, of course) is "no time." If I gave my children as much time as I give God, I could be prosecuted for child neglect and abuse. If I spent as little time with my wife as I spend with God, she'd have grounds for divorce for desertion.

Yet we all know from experience that when we give God time, we are happy. When we cheat God, we cheat ourselves. We know this from thousands of repeated experiments. And yet we keep running away from God, from communion with God, from prayer, as if it were bitter medicine. We are so afraid of silence and solitude, which are necessary for private prayer, that we give it to our most desperate criminals as the most horrible torture our mind can conceive—"solitary confinement!"

Why don't we seem to have as much time as our ancestors? In

fact, we all have exactly the same amount: twenty-four hours each day. Technology should have given us scads of extra time. Our lives should be oozing with leisure. All those time-saving devices! Yet they've done exactly the opposite. The more time-saving devices we have, the less time we have. (The only way to get time is to turn the clock back, not forward!) What went wrong?

Our great-grandmothers took many hours to scrub their clothes on a hand-held washboard; we just push a button on a washing machine. Our forefathers had to grow, hunt, and slaughter their own food; we buy it at the supermarket, open the microwave door, and push a button. Yet we are far more harried and hassled by time than they were. Why?

In most ancient societies, the rich had slaves to do their manual work so that they could enjoy leisure. Today, machines have replaced slaves; yet we have less leisure, not more. Why?

This is not the place for a general diagnosis of our society's sickness (though for a quick, profound hint, read Pascal's *Pensées*, especially on "diversion"). But it *is* the place for a diagnosis of our excuse for not praying, and I think this diagnosis has many other applications too.

"All that we are begins with our thoughts; it moves as our thoughts move, and it ends where our thoughts end." So says Buddha, wisely. We must begin here with our *thoughts* about time. We don't have time for prayer because *we think wrongly* about time and prayer.

We have time and prayer backwards. *We think time determines prayer, but prayer determines time.* We think our lack of time is the cause of our lack of prayer, but our lack of prayer is the cause of our lack of time.

When a little boy offered Christ five loaves and two fishes, he multiplied them miraculously. He does the same with our time, but only if we offer it to him in prayer. This is literally miraculous, yet I know it happens from repeated experience. Every day that I say I am too busy to pray, I seem to have no time, accomplish little, and feel frazzled and enslaved by time. Every day that

I say I'm too busy ***not*** to pray, every time I offer some time-loaves and life-fishes to Christ, he miraculously multiplies them and I share his conquest of time. I have no idea ***how*** he does it, I know ***that*** he does it, time after time.

And yet I resist sacrificing my loaves and fishes to him. I am an idiot. That's one of the things original sin means: spiritual insanity, preferring misery to joy, little bits of hell to little bits of heaven.

We must restore our spiritual sanity. One giant step in that direction is to think truly about time.

Time is like the setting of a play. The setting is really part of the play, contained by the play, determined by the play. But we often think the opposite: We think the play is contained by the setting. We think that the theme, the meaning, the spirit of the play is ***in*** its material setting instead of the other way around.

That's like thinking the soul is in the body. In fact, the body is in the soul. So says St. Thomas Aquinas. And since time measures the movements of material bodies, while prayer measures the movements of the soul, time is really in prayer rather than prayer in time. Prayer determines and changes and miraculously multiplies time (the loaves and fishes).

But prayer multiplies time only if and when we sacrifice our time, offer it up. There's the rub. We fear sacrifice. It's a kind of death.

All the real religions of the world are based on sacrifice, on willing death. Only the fake religion of pop psychology (which has infiltrated even the modern church) ignores this fact. Even pagans and polytheists know it. The most popular god in India is Shiva, the Destroyer, and the most popular goddess is Kali, his female equivalent. Even Hindus know the importance of spiritual surgery, death, sacrifice. After Calvary, how can Christians know this any less? Our Lord repeatedly taught us that unless we took up our cross and followed him, we could not be his disciples.

This probably means some terrible and difficult things; but one of the simple and easy things it means is to sacrifice our ***time*** to God. For time is life—"life-time."

The point is very simple: In order to create time to pray, we must destroy time to do something else. We must kill something, refuse something, say no to something.

To what? Let me make a simple, obvious, radical suggestion: the TV. Kill the TV. Go cold turkey for a month. I dare you. If you can't do that, then TV is your drug and you're an addict. "A man is a slave to whatever he cannot part with that is less than himself," said George MacDonald.

Every single person and family I know who has done this (voluntarily) has been very happy about it.

TV is largely a sewer pipe anyway; why fill your brain and your soul with the waste products from the most bigotedly antireligious elite in our society? Even if there were nothing to sacrifice TV *for*, it would be good to sacrifice it, to save your moral sanity and intelligence. All the more reason to sacrifice it for prayer. Find out how many hours a week you watch TV and use just half of that time for prayer. You get a threefold benefit: garbage cleanup, prayer time, and extra time left over.

The alternative is the mental slavery we see around us, the juggernaut—the worrying and rushing and never getting there because "there" is not in time at all, but in eternity. The modern world is unhappy because it does not touch eternity. All true happiness is a foretaste of eternity.

Eternity is not in the future but in the present. The future is unreal, not yet real. One of the devil's most ridiculous and successful lies is the idea that we should devote our lives to pursuing and acquiring goods we do not yet have rather than enjoying the ones we do have. This makes us slaves to time, to the unreal future, forever, for "tomorrow is always a day away."

The first rule for prayer, the most important first step, is not about *how* to do it, but to *just do it;* not to perfect and complete it but to begin it. Once the car is moving, it's easy to steer it in the right direction, but it's much harder to start it up when it's stalled. And prayer is stalled in our world.

So stop reading and start praying. Right now.

FIFTEEN

Boredom

Believe it or not, this is the one topic I always get the most interest and attention from in my philosophy classes whenever it comes up. No passage in the history of philosophy seems to touch their lives more than Pascal's observations in the *Pensées* on boredom, diversion, and indifference.

Every serious social problem that is tearing our society, our families, and our lives apart today—drugs, promiscuity, violence, infidelity, divorce—can be explained by this motive.

The main cause of war is boredom. People who are busy and happy do not fight wars. Think: When the Gulf War started, weren't you suddenly very, very *interested* in the news for the first time in years?

Here is an amazing fact: "The word *boredom* did not enter the language until the eighteenth century. No one knows its etymology," according to the acclaimed novelist Walker Percy in *Lost in the Cosmos.*

Almost the same thing can be said of atheism: It hardly existed at all before the eighteenth century.

The relation between the two is evident: Only God and the

attributes of God—love, wisdom, beauty, joy, holiness—are infinite and inexhaustible; therefore without God everything is eventually boring.

Weren't people bored before the eighteenth century? They got tired of cutting wood for ten hours, but they didn't get tired of *everything*. That's what boredom means.

The only possible explanation for this modern madness is this: It is not the world that is boring, but the self. Since it simply isn't true that everything real, everything in objective reality, is boring, therefore the source of boredom must be within. The bored self is projecting its own inner emptiness out onto reality.

Many people think that those who don't get easily bored are shallow, simple, and naïve, while those who do get easily bored are more deep, profound, and sophisticated. This is exactly the opposite of the truth. The bored self is not a big self in a little world. It is a little self in a big world. It reduces the big world to a small world by projecting its own littleness onto its world.

Boredom never comes *to* a self, only *from* a self—from a self that feels itself as empty, meaningless, and purposeless. Its inner emptiness sucks out the fullness and beauty of the world, like a black hole.

When the Jews in the Auschwitz concentration camp had to build things for their Nazi tormentors, working sixteen hours a day in pain, hunger, and freezing cold, no one was bored. Then the Nazis made them work at random and meaningless tasks, lifting heavy loads from one place to another and then back again. Then many of the prisoners went mad and committed suicide.

Viktor Frankl was a Jewish (later Catholic) psychiatrist in Auschwitz. In his great little classic *Man's Search for Meaning*, he tells how he discovered there that the deepest need of the human heart is not for pleasure or power or even freedom, but meaning and purpose. Those who had this, survived; those who did not, died.

Thousands of contemporary hospital patients who were seemingly dead but were resuscitated (usually by CPR) had hellish rather than heavenly out-of-body experiences. All of them reported the same thing: that hell was boring and purposeless. No one ***did*** anything. Everyone either sat around morosely or wandered about aimlessly, in a gray fog.

In other words, the modern world is becoming more and more like hell.

The only alternative to hell is heaven. Earth is merely the meeting point of the two, the battlefield between the two, the diving board into one of those two eternal swimming pools.

Heaven is not boring. In fact, ***only*** heaven (and heaven's colonies on earth) is not boring.

The church, the people of God, is heaven's colony on earth. The saints are never bored.

Therefore, the alternative to boredom, the cure for boredom, and the cure for all the ills of the modern world that are rooted in its boredom—is sanctity.

Sanctity—a relationship with God—is essentially letting God be present, letting heaven rule its colonies, establishing the kingdom of heaven on earth, in human hearts and human lives. Sanctity is essentially "the practice of the presence of God," as Br. Lawrence put it in the title of his little classic.

Saints "do all for the glory of God" (1 Cor 10:31). Sanctity is not only willing God's will, it is also thinking God's thoughts. We are to love God with our whole mind as well as our whole heart (Mt 22:37). Sanctity means seeing that everything has a purpose—in fact, that everything has the same purpose, that "all things work together for good" (Rom 8:28); and that that purpose is the most joy-filled, glory-weighted purpose any heart has ever imagined: receiving and giving back infinite, absolute, unconditional divine love forever.

If this vision—revealed by God through Scripture and church—is not true, it is the world's greatest fairy tale, lie, con job, and deception. There is no third possibility. The one thing it certainly is, is ***interesting***. The one thing it can't be is boring.

Saints are fanatics. They know this infinite thing. The rest of the world is bored because they know only finite things. So they use "fanatic" as their F-word. No one is less welcome in sophisticated modern society than a "fanatic," especially a "religious fanatic."

A temperature of 98.6 is a fever to a cold-blooded reptile. Modern man is evolving into a reptile: cold-blooded and passionless.

Cold-blooded reptiles also conform to the temperature of their environment—another new characteristic of modern man, who no longer believes in a natural law.

A doctor friend of mine spent three years in the jungles of Zaire, with an extremely primitive tribe, called primitive by others who, by contrast, supposedly live in a superior society. When he told them about life in so-called civilization, they believed everything, every technological wonder, except one thing: They literally could not believe that millions of American women killed their own unborn babies.

Humanity is evolving into a reptile. Only saints can save the world.

SIXTEEN

If I Were God...

Perhaps some day I'll write a book by that title. It would have to be a satirical, ironic piece of comic absurdity, because those are four of the silliest words we can say.

Why? Well, for one thing, they could hardly be more contrary to fact. The difference between you and God is far greater than the difference between you and a flea's eye. The first is infinite, the second finite.

A second reason those words are "silly to the max" is that it's stupid to ***want*** to be God. In fact, there is hardly anything more stupid. It's literally satanic—that was Satan's sin of pride.

You probably don't mean that when you say, "If I were God..." You probably mean only something like this: "It seems that God is doing a less than perfect job of running his world, and if I were in charge, I'd make some changes. I'd arrange for certain people who are doing the most harm to die quickly, and for people who are doing the most good to live long, healthy lives. I'd arrange for the Red Sox to win at least one World Series. I'd arrange for ten times as many people to read Catholic literature as read the secular press. Et cetera."

In other words, although our faith tells us that God knows what he's doing and that God's way is the best way and that all things work together for good, our reason and our eyes and our feelings all seem to tell us something different. So we naturally wonder, like Job, just why God does this or allows this or doesn't do that.

Wondering is natural and proper, and if we follow it to its logical conclusion, we may learn something. Let's try.

Let's follow out our wishes. Let's suppose we were God. Now let's imagine how we would improve the world. But let's not forget we have to pick up the pieces—that is, we'd be stuck with all the consequences of what we did. If all good were rewarded in an earthly and immediate way and all evil punished—if all the good people lived long and all the evil people died young, for instance—would there still be free choice between good and evil? And how hard would it be to choose good for good's sake alone, rather than for the sake of the earthly reward, if goodness always got an earthly reward?

If you were God and you turned all the bullets of all the murderers into butter before they entered the bodies of their innocent victims, would murderers still be able to choose between good and evil? If it became physically impossible to do evil and you started that policy of preventing all evil, wouldn't you have to follow it out to the end and perform a frontal lobotomy on every brain that threatened to conceive an evil thought?

It's amazing how wise and patient God is. If we were God, we wouldn't hold back our power, confronted with the horrible evils and injustices that prevail on earth. What wise restraint for God to act as if he didn't exist, to stay his hand!

When God answered Job's agonized question about evil, all he said was: "Where were you when I laid the foundations of the earth?" In other words, you can't do my job because you don't have my wisdom. Power without wisdom is the formula for disaster.

That is precisely the modern world: power without wisdom,

increase in power plus decrease in wisdom. Just when we have thrown away our old road maps, we have learned how to soup up the car.

One thing each of us can do about this social problem starts right in our own individual private lives: We can accept God's restrictions on our power. Like Paul, we can glory in our weaknesses.

Without weaknesses, we would be bored, dangerous, and proud. Bored, because it is only weakness and limits that create drama and heroism; it is only limits that create adventure. That's why the rich are bored: Their money makes them too close to omnipotent. And power is dangerous, because power corrupts, and makes us proud.

Isn't it a little disconcerting to realize that when we say "If I were God..." we never mean "If I were as loving as God..." but always "If I were as powerful as God"? Reflect on this.

Why do we think of power first whenever we think of God? Why do we say, "Almighty God" as if "Almighty" were his first name? If goodness is his essence, rather than power, why don't we spontaneously say "Good God"? Why have we reduced that to a piece of profanity, a taking of God's name in vain?

The obvious answer is that we are very stupid. Sin does that to us, makes us very stupid, deep down, in the heart. And that's why God can't trust us with much power.

We can become more like God only by becoming more loving, more good, more "weak." Then and only then will he trust us with power. Only when we learn to be weak will we be allowed to be strong. In heaven this will be perfected. But we must practice here.

Let's begin by remembering this: Every time we're tempted to say, "If I were God..." say instead, "Since I'm not God...." The rest of the sentence will be wiser, I guarantee you.

SEVENTEEN

Perfect Fear Casts Out "Luv"

Have you ever reflected seriously on the amazing fact that most of those who are called "religious educators" today deliberately try to eradicate from the souls of their students the very thing that the Bible calls "the beginning of wisdom"? I mean, of course, fear—"the fear of the Lord."

An army of modern psychologists is on the side of the educators rather than on the side of the Bible—at least, in America. For Americans desperately want to be wanted, like to be liked, need to be needed. ("People who need people are the luckiest people in the world," you know?)

Then, sometimes I think the situation couldn't possibly be that bad, that clear-cut. I must be misunderstanding these modern religious educators. Perhaps the fear they want to erase is not the fear the Bible speaks of at all. What they say is that the fear the Bible speaks of means only *respect,* and the fear the bad old days instilled was *terror.* Is this true? I think both parts of the claim are untrue.

First, what the Bible means by "the fear of the Lord" is far deeper than mere respect. You can have respect for policemen, and for debating partners, and even for money. But "the fear of the Lord" is something that takes its specific character from its object, from the Lord. It is awe. It is worship. It is wonder. It is absolute adoration. It is "islam," total "submission" to God. This is precisely the thing absent from both modern religious education and from modern liturgy. The reason is simple: You can't give what you don't have; you can't teach what you don't know yourself.

The second part of the claim is also false. The church did not instill terror in the past, nor is traditional religion based on terror. You have terror toward an enemy, like cancer, or a lion, or a bullet. It is a dead, dread, doomsday kind of feeling. "The fear of the Lord" is exultant and wonderful.

The church used to instill this awe. The main reason she is so weak and wimpy today is because she no longer instills this awe. For this awe is "the beginning of wisdom" and the heart of all true religion.

We have to distinguish three things, then, three kinds of fear: mere respect, awe, and terror. Awe is, in fact, closer to terror than to respect; for awe and terror have in common *passion* and *mystery.* Take passion and mystery out of religion and it becomes "psychobabble"—something lukewarm and nice, something flabby and flat and floppy and flaccid, like a wet noodle.

But doesn't the Bible say, "Perfect love casts out fear" (1 Jn 4:18)? And don't Jesus and the angels always tell us, "Fear not"? Yes, but *this* fear is terror. God would not tell us not to have "the beginning of wisdom"!

Terror is a bond, however primitive, between us and God. It is supposed to be there, and it is supposed to be cast out. It is supposed to be there because we are born original sinners, and the sinful self is naturally and rightly terrified of the goodness of God, which is sin's enemy. It is meant to be cast out because God saves us from sin, and then the relation changes from enemies to friends, and from terror to wonder.

"As long as there are wild beasts around, it is much better to feel fear (terror) than to feel secure," says George MacDonald.

If there is no fear for love to cast out, the love will not arrive as a great conqueror. If there are no dragons, a knight is just a big boy in a tin suit.

Love should cast out terror, but it should not cast out awe. True love includes awe. This is one of the great secrets of sex and marriage that our age has tragically forgotten: awe at the mystery that sex is. Science has not explained away this mystery, nor has psychology. No true mystery is ever explained away. Sex, death, love, evil, beauty, life, the soul, God—these remain forever infinite mysteries that we never exhaust and should not want to. They are like the ocean, for us to swim in, not like a glass of water for us to drink and drain dry.

God is love. And love is not "luv." Luv is nice; love is not nice. Love is a fire, a hurricane, an earthquake, a volcano, a bolt of lightning. Love is what banged out the big bang in the beginning, and love is what went to hell for us on the cross.

The difference between love and "luv" is the difference between the prophetic model of religion and the therapeutic model. In the prophetic model, God commands us to *be* good. In the therapeutic model, people use religion to make themselves *feel* good.

Not only are we missing something when fear is absent from religion, but (far worse) we are sinning grievously. For the absence of the fear of God is arrogance and pride. How dare sinners sashay up to God as a chum without first falling down in repentance and fear and calling on the Blood of Christ to save us?

This is not a private opinion; it is the teaching of the Bible, the church, and the saints. All the saints, who are far more advanced in love than we are (that's why they're saints), continued to have fear (awe) of God. They also continued to have terror-fear: not at God, but at sin. They often said things like: It would be better for the world to be destroyed than for one more sin to be committed. Things like: One sin is a thousand times worse than a thousand sufferings. Even the good pagan Socrates knew that "it is far better to suffer evil than to do it." He had a better understanding of the terror of sin than most modern Christians.

Christ himself told us to fear, and whom to fear: "Do not fear those who kill the body but cannot kill the soul; rather fear him who can destroy both soul and body in hell" (Mt 10:28).

If the thing we fear most is sin, then we will not fear death much, for after death we will no longer be able to sin. That's why the saints look forward to death instead of fearing it. It's a little evil, like a tourniquet or a quarantine; it prevents a far greater evil, like bleeding to death or an epidemic.

Islam has not lost this awe. That's why it's the world's fastest growing religion. Eastern Orthodoxy has not lost it as much as we have in the West. That's one reason why we need reunion with it. The pope often says the church has two lungs, East and West, and needs both to breathe. He has confided that reunion with the East is one of the three most important goals of his pontificate. (The other two are saving the world from nuclear war and cleaning up the church in America. One of these is much easier, the other much harder, than reunion with the East.)

Yes, "perfect love casts out fear." That is, *agape* casts out terror. But perfect fear also casts out "luv." Awe casts out "luv" as a hurricane casts out a teddy bear.

Perfect love casts out fear, but unless we begin with fear, we cannot progress to perfect love. Fear is the caterpillar; love is the butterfly.

EIGHTEEN

A Plea to Reinstate Adoration

When is the last time you saw an exposition of the Blessed Sacrament?

Why has devotion to the Blessed Sacrament declined exactly now, when there is greater need than ever before, now that we are engaged in full-scale cultural and spiritual warfare with the forces of antichrist that have emerged, like the beast from the sea in the Book of Revelation?

There are three main answers to this question.

First, people have less and less time. Leisure is a concept that is rapidly going the way of the concept of chastity. As our technological time-saving devices multiply, we are increasingly becoming enslaved to them, and to the people and forces that control them. It is genuinely harder today to take an hour for adoration than it ever was in the past. This fact alone proves that we are in serious decline.

Second, the sense of adoration is also in decline. The very experience of awe, wonder, and worship—the sense of the holy—

that is the psychological origin of all religion, seems to be absent in most Americans, Christian as well as secular, Catholics as well as Protestants. The category of "the holy" is disappearing because the experience of "the holy" is disappearing.

This disappearance was not brought about by outside, secular forces. It happened through spies and fifth columnists in the churches themselves, through some liturgists and catechists and seminary professors and middle management administrators and even some bishops. Who teaches us to adore any more?

A third reason for the decline of devotion to the Blessed Sacrament is even more simple and shocking: a decline of faith in it. According to a recent poll reported in *The National Catholic Register*, only 30 percent of Catholics even believe in the Real Presence anymore!

I am waiting with dread for the next poll, which may show that 70 percent of Catholics don't even believe Christ is divine.

Theological orthodoxy and intellectual faith are not sufficient, but they are necessary. Unless we believe that Christ is *true*, we cannot believe in *Christ*. Unless we *believe* that Christ is present in the Sacrament, we cannot *adore* him there, or feed off his Body.

Suppose you saw him there, literally, with your physical eyes. How would you feel? What would you say? What would you do? Why do you not feel, say, and do exactly the same things then, since he is just as truly and really present there as you are, though unseen?

Very great healing could come from the restoration of adoration—by restoration of the practice of exposition of the Blessed Sacrament.

The fundamental reason for this adoration must not be, however, anything practical and extrinsic to its own justice. It is just and right to do so: that is the reason for it. God must be adored not to win cultural battles, or even to restore orthodoxy, but simply because he deserves to be adored.

If we did this, four wonderful results would follow.

First, it would teach us to listen, and to be quiet, and to take time again. Perhaps even to ponder and contemplate, like Mary.

Second, it would teach us to time-travel, to transcend the present: to go back to the time of Christ's first coming, to become contemporary with Christ, to walk in his steps; and to go forward to the time of his second coming, to meet the one we must prepare to meet when death transforms time into eternity. The end of the world, the second coming, and the Last Judgment are not more than one hundred years away for anyone reading this chapter; for ***your*** end is your meeting with him who judges and ends time at ***the*** end.

(Isn't it strange that the doctrine that God judges—a doctrine found on almost every page of Scripture—is almost ***never*** preached today? Aren't the results obvious?)

Third, you will learn to adore by doing it. Adoration is like virtue: You learn only by practice.

Adoration is the essence of religion. When you adore, you know why religion is the most intense fire in human history—it is the opposite of boring. And it reveals your own deep heart at the time it reveals God; you meet and come to know him and yourself only together.

Fourth, it will teach you realism, to live in the real world, not a subjective fantasy world of slogans and ideologies. It will teach you the realism of faith. St. Thomas addressed Christ in the Blessed Sacrament this way:

> Sight, taste, and touch in Thee are each deceived;
> The ear alone most safely is believed:
> I believe all the Son of God has spoken:
> Than Truth's own word there is no truer token.

He is there. We must adore him because he is there. The fundamental reason for adoring God is not us but God. Adoration is self-forgetful. Yet we need to adore, while God does not need to be adored. We need to forget our needs.

We must adore. God commands it. The church commands it—not just ***commends*** it—but ***commands*** it.

We must adore because it is true. Adoration is the essence of sanity: it is the basic response to the basic fact. God is the basic fact. Adoration is the basic response. Sanity is essentially responding to fact.

Restoration of adoration of the Sacrament will heal our church, and thus our nation, and thus our world. It is one of Satan's most destructive lies that sitting alone in a dark church adoring Christ is irrelevant, impractical, a withdrawal from vital contemporary needs. Adoration touches everyone and everything in the world because it touches the Creator, who touches everything and everyone in the world from within, in fact, from their very center. When we adore, we plunge into the center of the hurricane, "the still point of the turning world"; we plug into infinite dynamism and power. Adoration is more powerful for construction than nuclear bombs for destruction.

And it's only as far away as our nearest church.

NINETEEN

What's New This Christmas?

The other day I heard for the first time something I had heard hundreds of times before.

It was a phrase from the canon of the Mass, dulled with familiarity. But the Spirit blew the dust and dullness off for a minute, and it flashed like sudden, sky-shattering lightning. It lit up my mind's sky and revealed Christmas. It showed Christmas in its true colors: as utterly unique, unexpected, surprising, shocking, stunning, and startling.

The line was: "the new and everlasting covenant."

I had never noticed the simple fact that there is nothing else in all reality that is both new *and* everlasting.

To see how shocking this is, contrast another phrase, one of the most obvious and un-shocking sayings ever said. It comes from Buddha, the primary teacher of half the world, the Eastern half. He called it "the pure and spotless eye of my Doctrine," that is, the principle he was most absolutely certain of: "Whatever is an arising thing, that is also a ceasing thing." In other words, whatever is born, dies. Whatever has a beginning, has an ending. What goes up must come down. What goes around, comes around.

In this vision of reality, all things in the river of time come and go and are swept away forever. Only the timeless, only nirvana, has no end, for it has no beginning and no time, no history. In this vision, there are only two kinds of reality: the temporal, which has both beginning and ending; and the eternal, which has neither.

How obvious this sounds! Like the fundamental law of nature. And it is just that. Yet it is *not* universally true. Christmas is the one exception to it. Christmas is the miracle that bursts and shatters apart the fundamental law of nature. At Christmas something comes into existence that will last forever.

The thing the priest calls "the new and everlasting covenant" directly contradicts Buddha's first law of nature; for here is an "arising thing" that is not also a "ceasing thing," something both new and everlasting.

In fact, there are no less than *five* things, or rather five aspects of this one thing, that are both new and everlasting.

First, there is the human body of Jesus Christ. He took it from Mary's yes at the Annunciation, and he took it to heaven in the Ascension. He has it now in heaven, and he will have it forever.

Second, there is his mystical body, the church—the body he left on earth, the people of God, us. The church will also last forever.

Third, each member of the church will receive a new, resurrection body like Christ's, which, like his, will be a real, concrete body, that has a beginning but has no ending and lives forever.

Fourth, our souls, which had a beginning in time (our conception), also have no end in time.

Fifth, the Eucharist, the "new and everlasting covenant" which the priest refers to in the Mass, also will last forever.

All five are aspects of the Body of Christ. All five begin in time and never end in time.

Christmas celebrates the beginning of these five things, for it celebrates the coming-to-be-in-time of Jesus, the baby who is born but never dies, the new body that never gets old.

No sage or saint, no madman or mystic, no philosopher or poet, no religionist or rationalist in the history of the world ever announced anything as wild, weird, and wonderful as this. It is indeed, as Kierkegaard calls it, "the absolute paradox." It is impossible. It is absurd. But our God is the God with whom all things are possible. He is the "Lord of the absurd."

Let us try to remember to be stupefied this Christmas as we see one of millions of reminders of this impossible thing, this everlasting baby. And let us remember also that every baby in every crib that we see now is, because of this one baby, invited to share in this same "impossibility."

Finally, let us remember that we in our anti-baby, anti-life, abortion-mad culture have an even more compelling reason for protecting babies than our natural hatred of murder: our supernatural marching orders, echoing eternally from this baby's mouth: "Truly, truly I say unto you, whatever you did to one of the least of these my brothers, you did to me."

TWENTY

The Vulgarity of Christmas

Do you find yourself complaining each Christmas at all the vulgar, tawdry, tasteless, cheap, and ugly things you see around you? Are you angry at the world for vulgarizing the most sublime event in history—next to the resurrection? If so, here is a little therapy for your anger: the thought that God deliberately designed Christmas—the first Christmas—as vulgar.

"Vulgar" means "common." It means the opposite of "sophisticated, stylish, aristocratic." The vulgarity of Christmas is a kind of sacrament or sign of the vulgarity of the Christian faith and of the Catholic church.

I have a number of good friends who were once Anglicans and are now Catholics. One of them calls his shabby local church "Our Lady of Perpetual Linoleum." He had been used to the most enchantingly lovely old stone English churches, the liturgy of the old Book of Common Prayer (surely the most beautiful liturgy in the history of the English language), and in general a church so tasteful that, as Ronald Knox said, "nobody in the whole world hates the Church of England." Now he is aboard the Catholic ark, full of animals. And it's not at all elegant.

God chose such an ark for himself when he came to earth. The manger is a miniature of Noah's ark. We must cut through our traditional tendency to romanticize the manger scene. Anyone who has lived on a farm knows what's in a stable. The primary smell is not a word accepted in polite company. We uprooted urban sophisticates often idealize farmers, peasants, stables, and even poverty—as long as it's country poverty instead of city poverty (because we *know* city poverty but not country poverty). We even romanticize the cow manure in the stable, for our experience of cow manure is from buying plastic packages of processed manure in garden shops for fertilizer!

I hope no one will interpret this thought as impious or unserious, but we should contemplate the fact that the only one who ever was able to choose his own place of birth chose a place full of manure. The incarnation does not mean some abstract doctrine about the intersection of eternity and time; the incarnation means that God stepped in our manure.

Noah's ark, a type of the church, must have been full of manure. (Have you ever been close to the cages in a zoo?) Job found wisdom and met God face to face from his *dung* heap. St. Paul used that word (skubala) to sum up all his worldly achievements and treasures when compared to "the surpassing worth of knowing Christ Jesus my Lord" (Phil 3:8). How vulgar God is! One can hardly imagine suburban ladies in white furs or city gentlemen in black Mercedes writing this way.

Christ was a commoner, from birth to death. He began in a borrowed cradle, he ended in a borrowed tomb. The church's "preferential option for the poor" is not an abstract ideology but a description of her Lord's life.

The saints, who are closer to us in time, help us understand that life. We understand the saints through Christ and we understand Christ through the saints. The saints are usually simple. Thomas Merton, in *Seven Storey Mountain*, tells that when he was thinking of becoming a Catholic, he discovered St. John of the Cross and was deeply impressed, but wondered whether it was the saint's sophistication and intelligence and style that were impressing him—so he deliberately read the writings of the *least* sophisticated, clever, and stylistic saint he knew, St. Thérèse, the Little Flower. To his joy and surprise he found the very same substance, the same reality of sanctity, behind the commonness of St. Thérèse as he had found on the mountainous heights of St. John of the Cross. I remember vividly how exactly my experience reduplicated his.

A sort of contemporary St. Thérèse is Mother Angelica. If you should ever happen by chance to turn to her TV program on Eternal Word Television Network (EWTN), you may be surprised and even put off a bit by her totally unstylish appearance, style, dress, format, and speech. But if you stay tuned for another minute, you sense the strength of simplicity, sanctity, and faith—and you are caught.

Being a saint means nothing more or less than being Christlike. Christ was not sophisticated or stylish. "He had no beauty that we should desire him. He was despised and rejected by men" (Is 53:2-3). He was not a renowned teacher of mysticism like Buddha. He was not a great political leader or conqueror like Alexander. He was not a philosopher or scholar like Aristotle.

Yet he had a higher style and grace and beauty. Mother Angelica is far more beautiful than Marilyn Monroe. In Christ and in his saints the beauty and wisdom and power of the world are shown up as ugliness, foolishness, and weakness. In him and in them God's power is demonstrated. As St. Paul says, "The foolishness of God is wiser than men and the weakness of God is stronger than men" (1 Cor 1:25). *That's* what's going on in a manure-filled stable in Bethlehem.

Please don't misunderstand: Christmas—a baby in a cow barn—is not an exaltation of ugliness or an excuse for tawdriness. No second-rate tables ever came from a certain carpenter's shop in Nazareth. Jesus was "full of grace and truth" (Jn 1:14), like a great ballet dancer. No one ever had more "class" than Jesus. But it was the "class" not of the "upper class," but of a perfect slave.

I remember vividly the shock on the faces of some scholars at a conference overseeing a new Bible translation when I suggested that the best translation of ***doulos*** in Philippians 2:7 was not just "servant" but "slave," and further suggested that if Jesus had come to earth in America in 1800 he probably would have come as a black slave. I don't know who was more shocked: they at my suggestion or I at their shock.

When he comes to us now, he comes under an even lower form than a slave: the form of a little piece of bread, to be crushed by our teeth, mingled with our spittle, and swallowed like Jonah by the whale. *That's* his style, his "class"—always washing his disciples' feet, like a slave.

So when you see the washed-out face without make-up on that old Salvation Army lady on the street corner this Christmas; when you grimace at the dull, pedestrian translation of the liturgy that some unpoetic bishops forced on us two decades ago; when you see the cheap Santas and tinsel everywhere—remember that the God who invented galaxies and archangels also invented the Church of Our Lady of Perpetual Linoleum, and cow manure. He came into both on Christmas because of the vulgarity and commonness of his love.

PART FOUR

Good and Evil

TWENTY-ONE

When a Christian Sins

Christ was born into a world of sinners and left the world freed from sin—but still very sinful.

It's far worse when a Christian sins than when an unbeliever sins, in one sense. For a Christian knows the horror of sin. A Christian has seen Calvary.

But in another sense, it's far worse when an unbeliever sins. For an unbeliever *hasn't* seen the horror of sin, and will therefore be slower to repent.

What is our attitude supposed to be after we fall into sin? Br. Lawrence, in *The Practice of the Presence of God*, says that each time he falls into sin he turns to God and says: "See? Thus shall I always do if You do not give me the grace." And then, he says, he just turns resolutely away from his past sins, knowing the power of Christ's forgiving blood, and faces the future, not the past, starting all over again.

I think this is a far healthier attitude than most of us have. It is neither wallowing in guilt nor cavalierly ignoring sin. It is both humble (unlike cavalierly ignoring sin) and happy (unlike wallowing in guilt).

St. Paul says something very much like what Br. Lawrence says: "I know that in me, that is in my flesh, dwells no good thing" (Rom 7:18). But he also knows that his true self now is not his "flesh," or "old man," inherited from Adam. He is "in the Spirit." He is a son of God. "If any one is in Christ he is a new creation" (2 Cor 5:17).

This makes sin *more* horrible, because we have taken this new creation of God's, this Christ-life in us, and sinned with it. When a Christian steals, kills, or commits adultery, he makes Christ to steal, kill, or commit adultery! This is the shocking thing St. Paul says in 1 Corinthians 6:15-16.

But being a Christian also makes sin *less* horrible, for the Savior from sin, the Great Physician, is more present and ready with a cure than we are with the disease.

What should be our attitude after we sin? Not a cavalier "Oh, it's no big deal." Not a guilt complex either. And not a wishy-washy compromise between the two extremes, a little cavalier and a little guilty.

We who have seen the cross have seen the incomparable horror of sin. One sin is worse than a cosmic catastrophe. One soul disease is worse than a billion body diseases.

At the same time, we—like Br. Lawrence—can have a cheerful hope, faith, confidence, and optimism that must scandalize mere moralists. For we know the Savior.

Before we sin the devil wants us to think only about God's mercy and forgiveness, not about his justice and judgment and sin's horror. He wants us to be cavalier then. But after we sin, he wants us to feel despairingly guilty, to think only about justice and judgment and sin's horror, not God's mercy and love.

It is just as hard to resist the devil after we sin as before. And it is just as necessary. For despair is as deadly to our souls as pride.

Br. Lawrence says, "Thus shall I always do if You do not give me the grace." Well, then, why doesn't he give us the grace?

One answer comes from St. Francis, in the *Little Flowers:* "Tell me, brother, who, think you, is the readier: our God to give grace or we to receive it?"

But our very choice to receive and accept and cooperate with God's grace to overcome sin is itself dependent on God's grace, as St. Thomas says in his Treatise on Grace in the *Summa*. Grace is always first. Grace is not God's response to us; grace is the origin of our response to him.

Why, then, doesn't God give us sufficient grace to overcome sin? He could, and sometimes he does, but sometimes he doesn't. We know this from experience. There were times when we were not particularly holy, yet God gave us the grace to overcome sin. There were other times when we had a holy mind and a strong and loving intention, yet fell into sin. We know from experience that it is only partly our choice that makes the difference; the other factor is God's grace. Why does he sometimes withhold it?

St. Thomas gives one reason in the *Summa*:

> In order to overcome their pride, God punishes certain men by allowing them to fall into sins of the flesh, which though they are less grievous are more evidently sinful.... From this indeed the gravity of pride is made manifest. For just as a wise physician, in order to cure a worse disease, allows the patient to contract one that is less dangerous, so the sin of pride is shown to be more grievous by the very fact that, as a remedy, God allows men to fall into other sins.

Pride is the deadliest of the deadly sins, the devil's own sin, the thing that makes it eternally impossible to endure or enjoy God's heavenly presence. But pride is usually masked. Proud people often think they're humble. They may even be proud of their humility. It's humble people who think they're proud—too proud. Proud people think they're humble enough. Sinners think they're saints, and saints know they're sinners. Sin masks itself. The worst sins mask themselves the most: pride, hypocrisy, coldness, self-righteousness.

So God withholds grace to avoid some plain and obvious, non-respectable, unmasked fault like lust, drunkenness, cowardice, or addiction to keep us from pride. The key, then, to overcoming all sins is humility.

God will do *anything* to teach us this lesson, the lesson of our total, absolute, infinite, unqualified dependence on him.

Therefore the more we learn this lesson on our own, the less we'll need to learn it the hard way, by falling into other sins.

Perhaps that's why St. Augustine, when asked to name the four cardinal virtues, replied: "Humility, humility, humility, and humility."

Humility is not worminess or smarminess. It's not an attitude toward yourself at all, but an attitude toward God. It's self-forgetful.

It's the opposite of pride, which is also an attitude toward God. *Vanity* is an attitude toward yourself (thus "vanity *mirrors*"). Vanity is a minor vice compared to pride. Pride says no to God. Pride sings Sinatra's song, the song they sing in hell: "I did it my way."

Humility is a little baby crying because it just pooped in its pants. It's crying to mommy to change its diaper.

We're like that before God.

And he always changes us and makes us clean again.

To quote another song, this time a heavenly one, "All you have to do is call, and I'll be there... you've got a friend."

TWENTY-TWO

A Day without Sin?

"Deign, O Lord, to keep us this day without sin." The phrase from an old prayer comes to mind, and troubles me. I find things that trouble me mentally to be the very best things to think about. Only troubles make us grow, whether we speak of physical growth (exercise), mental growth (puzzles), or spiritual growth (sufferings and temptations).

Now what troubles me about that phrase? This: Is it *possible* for us to be sinless for a day? Are we ever sinless for a day?

We seem to be in a dilemma here. If we say yes, we put ourselves on a level with Mary if only for a day. If we say no, we make our efforts a sham. For if it is impossible to succeed, why try?

To solve this dilemma, we need to make a distinction. There are two kinds of sin, original and actual. We are freed from original sin by baptism. So it *is* possible to be sinless for a day—for a lifetime, in fact—if we speak of original sin. But what about actual sin?

I think it must be possible to live for one day without actual sin. Prayer is not pointless. The church does not give us pointless prayers. So her traditional prayer which I quoted at the beginning of the chapter must be one which can be answered. If not, if sin inevitably permeates everything we do, then we are left with a vague sense of guilt rather than a specific sense of sin—a Freudian guilt or a Woody Allen guilt instead of a Christian guilt.

This vague sense of guilt is a very common condition, I think, especially among Irish Catholics, Calvinists, and religious Jews. Apparently pious and humble, this sense of inevitable, all-penetrating sin is really the opposite. It gets us "off the hook" for actual, specific sins (which we are personally responsible for since we can avoid them) and transfers our guilt from specific choices to a vague, unspecific, all-permeating state which is little more than a *feeling*, which we cannot avoid and hence are not really personally responsible for.

The church, in her practical wisdom, commands us to confess specific sins. This presupposes that we can discover them and resolve to amend them. The resolution to amend them means that we *can* amend them, even if they are sins that stem from deeply ingrained habits, like alcoholism or homosexuality. What an optimistic compliment the church gives to our freedom here!

Yes, we *can* live a day without sin. How, then, do we differ from Mary?

First, the *habits* left in us from original sin, even after baptism, were not in her. She was not born with original sin.

Second, she went far beyond just avoiding sin. She practiced heroic virtue, works of supererogation. In other words, she did *more* than was required, and in a sort of spill-over effect, merited great graces for others, for us. All the saints did this to some extent. They lived lives of heroic virtue. We can too.

But not doing so is not something to feel *guilty* about, but *impatient* about. Guilt is meant to be like pain in the body; it has a specific purpose: to move us to avoid real, specific dangers. The feeling of impatience at our slow progress, the feeling that we have not done all that we could, the feeling of desire to be more heroic—these are good feelings, but they are not *guilt* feelings.

We also often confuse not doing works of heroism with sins of omission, and this also makes us feel wrongly guilty. Sins of omission are specific. Not doing heroic things is not. If you don't help the drowning child, that is a sin of omission. But if you don't become a foreign missionary, that is not.

If we refuse to let our sense of guilt go where it has no right to go—out into the wasteland of the general—it will do its rightful job: pointing out the dirty spots at home, those humdrum little sins we *can* clean up.

Most of us have a long, long way to go before we can be sinless for a day, except by a miracle. But it is a realistic and attainable goal. And then "one day at a time."

TWENTY-THREE

The Two Most Revolutionary Verses in the Bible

What do you think are the two most revolutionary, powerful, life-changing verses in the Bible for Christians today?

What do you think God most wants Christians to know and appreciate and live today?

It would be in the Bible because the Bible is God's complete data bank for all time that the church computes from. She enlarges her "deposit of faith" from within, like growing a seed, not from without, like adding a new wing onto a building.

Probably the most important verse in the Bible for ***unbelievers*** is John 3:16. But what about believers? What about believers ***today***?

Today is very different from yesterday, even a yesterday as recent as the 1950s. I ask for *two* verses because the church is sadly split today into right and left, conservatives and liberals, traditionalists and progressives. What does each need most? What does God want each to know?

How could we possibly know what God wants? Only because

God has already told us. That's what the Bible is. If we immerse ourselves in his Word, we get to know the One who speaks there—his character and will and strategy—and we get "the big picture." And that "big picture" gives us the perspective to guess intelligently at what's most needed now.

So how would you answer that question? What would your two verses be?

I'll tell you mine, and also the reason for my selection, and then you can apply it to yourself. If the shoe fits, wear it.

First we need to know we are split—what a conservative is and what a liberal is. We need to diagnose the disease before we can prescribe its cure.

Sometimes humor teaches best and says the most in the least words. Each of the following witty definitions makes a serious point.

1. "A conservative is one who is enamored of existing evils; a liberal is one who wishes to replace them with new ones." (Ambrose Bierce)
2. A liberal is someone who doesn't believe in evil, except for the evil in conservatives. A conservative is someone who *does* believe in evil—except for the evil in conservatives.
3. A conservative is a liberal who just got mugged. A liberal is a conservative who just got arrested.
4. A liberal and a conservative were scheduled to exchange their brains and their hearts in an experimental operation. But no one could find a conservative who would give up his heart, or a liberal who had any brains to give.

What do these political jokes have to do with our daily walk with God? They show one thing that gets in the way: political partisanship, political categories. The saints are neither liberals nor conservatives; they're Christians. They're little Christs. They're like Christ. They don't fit political categories. Christ was hated by both the right *and* the left of his day—by the dogmatic Pharisees and the skeptical Sadducees, by the Herodian collaborators and the Zealot revolutionaries.

For Christ, being perfect man, had a perfect head ***and*** a perfect heart, a perfectly hard head and a perfectly soft heart. He practiced what he preached about being wise as a serpent and harmless as a dove. One thread running through the definitions above is the double point about head and heart. We need a conservative head and a liberal heart.

The strong point of conservatives is that they conserve. They are faithful. They keep the faith. They are anchored in the faith. Their weak point is that they tend to be pugnacious and angry and graceless and merciless and loveless.

The strong point of liberals is their soft heart, their compassion. Their weak point is their soft head, their lack of principles, faith, fidelity, and anchors. They are strong on mercy, but weak on justice and on objective and unchanging moral principles—strong on love but weak on truth.

But both love and truth are absolutes. For they are eternal attributes of God. And in God they are not divided at all, but ***one thing***. That's why Jesus was both tough and gentle at once. He is a true gentleman, both gentle and manly, like a medieval knight. This is what every woman's heart desires in a man. It's also what every man desires in a woman. It's the kind of love that's designed to last a lifetime.

The saints, being little Christs, also have two absolutes: truth and love. They have hard heads and soft hearts. Mother Teresa and Pope John Paul II are good examples. Listen to them, not the media stereotypes of them, and you will see the pope's soft heart as well as his hard head, and Mother Teresa's hard head as well as her soft heart.

So now we know the patient and the disease. What's the prescription? What verse would God want every conservative to meditate on and pray over for a month? And what verse for every liberal?

Here's my guess. First, for the liberal: "The fear of the Lord is the beginning of wisdom" (Ps 111:10).

That's lesson one. Without it, no lesson two. The very things liberals try to eradicate from religious education—fear, holy fear, awe, wonder, and worshipful submission—is the very foundation of all religious education, all wisdom. With this holy fear go all the rest of the things liberals miss: supernaturalism, miracles, authority, obedience, absolutes, distinctiveness, hierarchy, ***height***.

A great rabbi, Abraham Heschel, said, "God is not ***nice***. God is not an uncle. God is an earthquake." Anyone who meets God knows that. Only experts and professors deny it. Anyone who meets the real God as distinct from the comfortable Chum invented by middle management bureaucrats and administrators "falls at his feet as though dead," as John did in Revelation 1:17. Liberals must learn to die that blessed death. For God announces that "no one can see me and live" (Ex 33:20).

Conservatives too must learn to die, a different kind of death: to smugness and satisfaction and "dead orthodoxy." Their verse is Matthew 25:40: "Truly, truly I say to you, as you did it to one of the least of these my brethren, you did it to me."

Suppose we really, really believed that? How would our lives change? Suppose we learned to really see Jesus Christ in the poorest of the poor, as Mother Teresa does—in the homeless bum and the schizophrenic and the AIDS patient, and even in the drug addict and the criminal and the sodomite. How would we respond to him or her? Would we pass the person by, like the priest and the Levite, or would we be good Samaritans? How would that change our lives?

The fear of the Lord is the beginning of wisdom. But it is not the end. Love is the end. Faith is the root, but love and the works of love are the fruit of the plant that is the Christ-life. If conservatives forget the social gospel, they forget the greatest thing of all, for "the greatest of these is love" (1 Cor 13:13). The son who said the wrong words but did his father's will is not as bad as the son who said the right words but didn't do them (Mt 21:28-31).

Only God can teach these two lessons. Liberals can't teach conservatives to love. Only the Holy Spirit can. Pray to the Holy Spirit to teach both, and to heal the terrible tear in the body of

Christ today. And pray that he teach you what you most need. Meditate on the verse you need most every day for a month, and see how your life changes. Then you will see how the world can be changed.

TWENTY-FOUR

Romans 8:28– Our Fortress

When a battle is not going well, the army retreats to a strong place, perhaps a fortress. When life is not going well, Christians have many fortresses. Those fortresses are found in Scripture. I would like to look at my favorite fortress in Scripture.

My fortress is not emotional but intellectual. It is not a passage designed to make us *feel* good but to assure our minds that no matter how bad we feel, reality *is* good.

The verse is Romans 8:28, one of the most familiar and beloved verses in the Bible. The old, literal King James Version of the Bible says: "And we know that all things work together for good to them that love God, to them who are called according to his purpose."

I have always thought this was one of the most startling, incredible things ever written. It certainly does not *look* like all things work together for good. Countless horrible examples leap to mind, like lizards leaping from a pit. What about *this*? What about *that*? *All* things?

First off, the fact that this flies in the face of appearances should not be surprising. If the Bible only told us what we already knew by our own senses, our own experience, and our own reasoning, it would be superfluous, uninteresting, and certainly no divine revelation. God only tells us what we need to hear, not what we already know. Faith always goes beyond both reason and feeling; otherwise, it would not be faith. We would have no need for it.

We can approach a verse like this, a verse that flies in the face of appearances, in two ways. We can either start with the appearances and try to interpret the verse in the light of these appearances; or we can start with the verse and interpret appearances in light of it.

If we do the first, we will almost certainly conclude that the verse is either pure myth and fantasy, or exaggeration, or an outright lie, or a psychological puff piece written to perk us up, like "everything's going to be all right" to a dying man in a panic. It may take away his panic, but it will not stop his dying.

I fear there is a strong tendency today among believers as well as unbelievers to reinterpret Scripture's hard sayings as puff pieces, subjective instead of objective, feelings instead of facts. I wonder how much of this is behind what I am told is now the growing consensus among "Scripture scholars" that Jesus' resurrection was not a literal, physical fact.

Here is what I do with Romans 8:28. I review my premises, what I stand on: first, my decision to believe in Christ. Can I cop out on that? No way. Next: my decision to believe in the visible church he established to communicate his message to me. Can I drop that? No, for if I do, I am stuck with my own very unreliable experience and calculations about him. The church is my lifeline to him. Next: the Bible, the book the church wrote, canonized, and stands on. If I believe the church, I must believe her book—all of it, not just those passages that give me no trouble or surprise or correction. So this verse, like every verse in the book, is as true, as divinely inspired, as providentially provided, and as free from error as any other verse in the book.

Therefore, it is true. If God says grass is purple and my eyes say it is green, I will believe the author of my eyes rather than my eyes. If God says Job's dung heap is really God's compassion, and Job's nerve endings say it is God's curse, I will believe God rather than nerve endings. This applies to mine—my dung heaps and my nerves—as well as Job's.

Having decided that "God said it, I believe it, and that settles it," I now—only now—try to make sense of it. This investigation is not a trial. The verse is not on trial. If I fail to make sense of it, I will still believe it. But I would like to make sense of it too, if I can.

I think I can. Reason backs up faith here. How?

There are three attributes of God that are very clear in Scripture. I think all three can be proved by good philosophical reasoning too. They are the minimum three attributes required for anyone to be called "God." Any being lacking in any one of these three attributes would not deserve the title "God" from any theist: Jewish, Christian, Muslim, or just a good rational philosopher.

The three attributes: (1) omnipotence, (2) omniscience, and (3) omnibenevolence. That is, God can do and control everything, God knows everything, and God wills every good. There is no weakness, ignorance, or bad will in God—not any at all.

Now, if God, the Creator of everything that exists except himself, is in total control of everything, knows what is ultimately best for me, and wills what is best for me, then everything that happens to me must be for my best good, ultimately. Romans 8:28 does not say that everything *is* good—that is obviously false—but that everything "works together" or works out for good, ultimately, in the long run.

Even evil. That's clear from *Job*. God lets Satan buffet Job just so far. God lets Job suffer just so long. God tells Job at the end that he controls Behemoth and Leviathan (primeval monsters, symbols of the forces of evil).

So whether it's a hemorrhoid or a holocaust, a dust storm or a divorce, God deliberately allows it to happen to me for one and only one reason: he loves me.

There's no way out. I'm hemmed in behind and before (Ps 139:5). Everything is his touch, sometimes pleasant, sometimes painful.

I have only two choices if I am honest. I can believe in the whole ball of wax, including Romans 8:28, or throw it all away. It's all one ball. And since I can't throw it all away, I have to believe this crazy thing, this thing all the saints went crazy with—crazy with wonder and love and joy and power and peace.

It's logical, it's inescapable. If God is omniscient, omnipotent, and omnibenevolent, all things work together for my good; if all things do not work together for my good, then such a God does not exist.

You see, reason can help faith a lot.

Of course, we have to read the whole verse. It announces this great truth only for those who love God, who are called to fulfill his purpose, that is, salvation. It does not apply to those who are eternally lost. Hell does not work together for anyone's good.

But repentance does. Even sins in a believer's life can come under this verse, through the golden door of repentance. Every time I sin, I miss a greater good that would have come to me by not sinning, but I can still attain a great good by repenting and learning from my sins. This is, I think, essentially the great good I will complete in purgatory.

And it doesn't say everything *feels* good, or that everything *is* good, just that everything *works together* for good, or works out for good in the long run, not necessarily in the short run. Perhaps the *long* run is only heaven, not on earth; perhaps the good that comes my way from some earthly evil will become evident only then, when God fills the hole in my heart that he has hollowed out by earthly suffering with his heavenly water. The bigger the hole, the bigger the waves.

TWENTY-FIVE

Discernment

Does God have one right choice for me in each decision I make?

When we pray for wisdom to discern God's will when it comes to choosing a mate, a career, a job change, a move, a home, a school, a friend, a vacation, how to spend money, or any other choice, big or little, whenever there are two or more different paths opening up before us and we have to choose, does God always will one of those paths for us? If so, how do we discern it?

Many Christians who struggle with this question today are unaware that Christians of the past can help them from their own experience. Christian wisdom embodied in the lives and teachings of the saints tells us two things that are relevant to this question.

First, they tell us that God not only knows and loves us in general but that he cares about every detail of our lives, and we are to seek to walk in his will in all things, big and little.

Second, they tell us that he has given us free will and reason because he wants us to use it to make decisions. This tradition is exemplified in Saint Augustine's famous motto "Love God and [then] do what you will." In other words, if you truly love God and his will, then doing what you will, will, in fact, be doing what God wills.

Do these two pieces of advice pull us in opposite directions, or do they only seem to? Since there is obviously a great truth embodied in both of them, which do we emphasize the most to resolve our question of whether God has one right way for us?

I think the first and most obvious answer to this question is that it depends on which people are asking it. We have a tendency to emphasize one half of the truth at the expense of the other half, and we can do that in either of two ways. Every heresy in the history of theology fits this pattern: for instance, emphasizing Christ's divinity at the expense of his humanity or his humanity at the expense of his divinity; or emphasizing divine sovereignty at the expense of free will or free will at the expense of divine sovereignty.

Five general principles of discernment of God's will that apply to all questions about it, and therefore to our question too, are the following:

1. *Always begin with data,* with what we know for sure. Judge the unknown by the known, the uncertain by the certain. Adam and Eve neglected that principle in Eden and ignored God's clear command and warning for the devil's promised pig in a poke.

2. *Let your heart educate your mind.* Let your love of God educate your reason in discerning his will. Jesus teaches this principle in John 7:17 to the Pharisees. (Would that certain Scripture scholars today would heed it!) They were asking how they could interpret his words, and he gave them the first principle of hermeneutics (the science of interpretation): "If your will were to do the will of my Father, you would understand my teaching." The saints understand the Bible better than the theologians, because they understand its primary author, God, by loving him with their whole heart and their whole mind.

3. *Have a soft heart but a hard head.* We should be "wise as serpents and harmless as doves," sharp as a fox in thought but loyal as a dog in will and deed. Soft-heartedness does not

excuse soft-headedness, and hard-headedness does not excuse hard-heartedness. In our hearts we should be "bleeding-heart liberals" and in our heads "stuck-in-the-mud conservatives."

4. *All God's signs should line up,* by a kind of trigonometry. There are at least seven such signs: (1) Scripture, (2) church teaching, (3) human reason (which God created), (4) the appropriate situation, or circumstances (which he controls by his providence), (5) conscience, our innate sense of right and wrong, (6) our individual personal bent or desire or instincts, and (7) prayer. Test your choice by holding it up before God's face. If one of these seven voices says no, don't do it. If none say no, do it.
5. *Look for the fruits of the spirit,* especially the first three: love, joy, and peace. If we are angry and anxious and worried, loveless and joyless and peaceless, we have no right to say we are sure of being securely in God's will. Discernment itself should not be a stiff, brittle, anxious thing, but—since it too is part of God's will for our lives—loving and joyful and peace-filled, more like a game than a war, more like writing love letters than taking final exams.

Now to our question. Does God have just one right choice for me to make each time? If so, I must find it. If not, I should relax more and be a little looser. Here are some clues to the answer.

The answer depends on what kind of person you are. I assume that many readers of this book are (1) Catholic, (2) orthodox and faithful to the teachings of the church, (3) conservative, and (4) charismatic. I have had many friends—casual, close, and very close—of this description for many years. In fact, I fit the description myself. So I speak from some experience when I say that people of this type have a strong tendency toward a certain character or personality type—which is in itself neither good nor bad—which needs to be nourished by one of these emphases more than the other. The opposite personality type would require the opposite emphasis.

My first clue, based on my purely personal observation of this kind of people, is that we often get bent out of human shape by our desire—in itself a very good desire—to find God's perfect will for us. We give a terrible testimony to non-Christians; we seem unable to relax, to stop and smell God's roses, to enjoy life as God gives it to us. We often seem fearful, fretful, terribly serious, humorless, and brittle—in short, the kind of people that don't make a very good advertisement for our faith.

I am not suggesting that we compromise one iota of our faith to appeal to unbelievers. I am simply suggesting that we be human. Go watch a ball game. Enjoy a drink—just one—unless you're at risk for alcoholism. Be a little silly once in a while. Tickle your kids—and your wife. Learn how to tell a good joke. Read Frank Schaeffer's funny novel *Portofino*. Go live in Italy for a while.

Here's a second clue. Most Christians, including many of the saints, don't, in fact, have the discernment we are talking about, the knowledge of what God wills in every single choice. It's rare. Could something as important as this be so rare? Could God have left almost all of us so clueless?

A third clue is Scripture. It records some examples—most of them miraculous, many of them spectacular—of God revealing his particular will. But these are reported in the same vein as miracles: as something remarkable, not as general policy. The "electronic gospel" of health and wealth, "name it and claim it," is unscriptural, and so is the notion that we must find the one right answer to every practical problem, for the same reason: We are simply never assured such a blanket promise. Darkness and uncertainty are as common in the lives of the saints, in Scripture as well as afterwards, as pain and poverty are. The only thing common to all humanity is that the gospel guarantees to free us from is sin (and its consequences, death, guilt, and fear), not suffering ***and not uncertainties***. If God had wanted us to know the clear, infallible way, he surely would have told us clearly and infallibly.

A fourth clue is something God did in fact give us: free will. Why? There are a number of good reasons—for instance, so that our love could be infinitely more valuable than instinctive, unfree animal affection. But I think I see another reason. As a teacher, I know that I sometimes should withhold answers from my students so that they find them themselves, and thus appreciate and remember them better—and also learn how to exercise their own judgment in finding answers themselves. "Give a man a fish and you feed him for a day; teach a man to fish and you feed him for a lifetime." God gave us some big fish, but he also gave us the freedom to fish for a lot of little ones (and some big ones) ourselves.

Reason and free will always go together. God created both in us as part of his image. He gives supernatural revelation to both: dogmas to our reason and commandments to our will. But just as he didn't give us all the answers, even in theology, in applying the dogmas or drawing out the consequences of them, so he didn't give us all the answers in morality or practical guidance, in applying the commandments and drawing out their consequences. He gave us the mental and moral equipment with which to do that, and he is not pleased when we bury our talent in the ground instead of investing it so that he will see how much it has grown in us when he returns.

In education, I know there are always two extremes. You can be too modern, too experimental, too Deweyan, too structureless. But you can also be too classical, too rigid. Students need initiative and creativity and originality too.

God's law is short. He gave us ten commandments, not ten thousand. Why? Why not a more complete list of specifics? Because he wanted freedom and variety. Why do you think he created so many persons? Why not just one? Because he loves different personalities. He wants his chorus to sing in harmony, but not in unison.

I know Christians who are cultivating ingrown eyeballs trying to know themselves so well—often by questionable techniques like the enneagram, or Oriental modes of prayer—so that they can make the decision that is exactly what God wants for them every time. I think it is much healthier to think about God and your neighbor more and yourself less, to forget yourself—follow your instincts without demanding to know everything about them. As long as you love God and act within his law, I think he wants you to play around a bit.

I'm happily haunted by Chesterton's image of the playground fence erected around the children on top of the mountain so that they could play without fear of falling off the side. That's why God gave us his law: not to make us worried but to keep us safe so that we could play the great games of life and love and joy.

Each of us has a different set of instincts and desires. Sin infects them, of course. But sin infects our reason and our bodies too; yet we are supposed to follow our bodily instincts (for example, hunger and self-preservation) and our mind's instincts (for example, curiosity and logic). I think he wants us to follow our hearts. Surely, if John loves Mary more than Susan, he has more reason to think God is leading him to marry Mary than Susan. Why not treat all other choices by the same principle?

I am not suggesting, of course, that our hearts are infallible, or that following them justifies sinful behavior. Nor am I suggesting that the heart is the *only* thing to follow. I mentioned seven guidelines earlier. But surely it is God who designed our hearts—the spiritual heart with desire and will as much as the physical heart with aorta and valves. Our parents are sinful and fallible guides too, but God gave them to us to follow. So our hearts can be worth following too even though they are sinful and fallible. If your heart loves God, it is worth following. If it doesn't, then you're not interested in the problem of discernment of his will anyway.

Here is a fifth clue. When we do follow Augustine's advice to "love God and then do what you will," we usually experience great relief and peace. Peace is a mark of the Holy Spirit.

I know a few people who have abandoned Christianity altogether because they lacked that peace. They tried to be super-Christians in everything, and the pressure was just unendurable. They should have read Galatians.

Here is a sixth clue. If God has one right choice in everything you do, then you can't draw any line. That means that God wants you to know which room to clean first, the kitchen or the bedroom, and which dish to pick up first, the plate or the saucer. You see, if you carry out this principle's logical implications, it shows itself to be ridiculous, unlivable, and certainly not the kind of life God wants for us—the kind described in the Bible and the lives of the saints.

Clue number six is the principle that many diverse things are good; that good is plural. Even for the same person, there are often two or more choices that are both good. Good is kaleidoscopic. Many roads are right. The road to the beach is right and the road to the mountains is right, for God awaits us in both places. Goodness is multicolored. Only pure evil lacks color and variety. In hell there is no color, no individuality. Souls are melted down like lead, or chewed up together in Satan's mouth. The two most uniform places on earth are prisons and armies, not the church.

Take a specific instance where different choices are both equally good. Take married sex. As long as you stay within God's law—no adultery, no cruelty, no egotism, no unnatural acts, as, for example, contraception—anything goes. Use your imagination. Is there one and only one way God wants you to make love to your spouse? What a silly question! Yet making love to your spouse is a great good, and God's will. He wants *you* to decide to be tender or wild, moving or still, loud or quiet, so that your spouse knows it's *you*, not anyone else, not some book who's deciding.

Clue number seven is an example from my own present experience. I am writing a novel for the first time, and learning how to do it. First, I placed it in God's hands, told him I wanted to do it for his kingdom, and trusted him to lead me. Then, I simply followed my own interests, instincts, and unconscious. I let the story tell itself and the characters become themselves. God doesn't stop me or start me. He doesn't do my homework for me. But he's there, like a good parent.

I think living is like writing a novel. It's writing the story of your own life and even your own self (for you shape your self by all your choices, like a statue that is its own sculptor). God is the primary author, of course, the primary sculptor. But he uses different human means to get different human results. He is the primary author of each book in the Bible too, but the personality of each human author is no less clear there than in secular literature.

God is the universal storyteller. He *wants* many different stories. And he wants you to thank him for the unique story that comes from your free will and your choices too. Because your free will and his eternal plan are not two competing things, but two sides of one thing. We cannot fully understand this great mystery in this life, because we see only the underside of the tapestry. But in heaven, I think, one of the things we will praise and thank God the most for is how wildly and wonderfully and dangerously he put the driving wheel of our life into our hands—like a parent teaching a young child to drive.

You see, we have to learn that, because the cars are much bigger in heaven. There, we will rule angels and kingdoms.

God, in giving us all free will, said to us: "Your will be done." Some of us turn back to him and say: "My will is that your will be done." That is obedience to the first and greatest commandment. Then, when we do that, he turns to us and says: "And now, *your* will be done." And then he writes the story of our lives with the pen strokes of our own free choices.

PART FIVE

Fantasies

TWENTY-SIX

Heaven's Dog

I had a dream.

I died, and approached the great judgment seat. I knew I would be judged by Omniscience, and therefore I could not quarrel with the judgment.

The first thing that was revealed to me from the Omniscience, by a kind of instant and unquestionable telepathy, was that God knew exactly what was in my unconscious mind as well as my conscious mind. He knew me better than I knew myself. I was not surprised at this. But then he revealed to me one of the things that had been in my unconscious mind, and this surprised me. Yet once I saw it, I knew it was true. Omniscience does not lie.

What I saw was my own unconscious expectations for this day of judgment. I had expected to go to heaven, to be saved, since I believed in the Savior. But I had also expected to be assigned a sort of middle position in heaven, neither high among the saints nor low among the rabble who just barely, surprisingly sneaked in by the skin of their teeth. I had not consciously realized before that this had been my unconscious expectation, but once the Omniscience revealed it to me, I recognized it as indeed what I had expected.

Then came the judgment. The first part was no surprise: I was to be granted entrance to heaven. All right. But the second part was quite a shock. I was the very lowest soul in heaven. *I* was the rabble. I had gotten in by the skinniest skin of my teeth.

This truth was put to me in an image. I do not know whether I was supposed to interpret the image literally or not, but it seemed literally real. I saw a great banquet hall, and saints small and great feasting at long tables, like a great medieval king's celebration. Where was my place, I wondered? Then I saw a mangy, skinny, gray, ugly, flea-bitten dog under the table, gobbling up scraps and bones thrown to him. The dog was also constantly kicked, playfully and thoughtlessly, by the high-spirited banqueters. It had to keep dodging out of the way, and was often unsuccessful, so that its body was full of bruises. For some reason, I was more fascinated by the dog than by the banqueters. Soon I understood why. That was me. If I accepted my proper place in heaven, it would be as that dog.

The vision of the banquet faded, and I realized I was now being offered an alternative. If I chose, I could be, instead of a dog at heaven's table, a prime minister in hell. I saw myself in the councils of hell, dressed in gold robes, admired by all, hell's greatest theologian, prophet, and guru—even hell's greatest saint! All other humans there were looking up to me. And as prime minister I would be in a position to sit in on hell's high (or low) councils and influence their decisions. I could soften or mitigate their evil work on earth. I could be heaven's spy in hell. It seemed I could do far more good in hell than in heaven, where I could only gobble up scraps and kicks from my superiors.

Hell, like heaven, seemed quite real, quite earthly, even physical. I saw no torture chambers, no fire and brimstone, only honors and influence. I would have a fine time in hell and a terrible time in heaven. I had to choose between being first in hell or last in heaven.

Then I remembered the verse from the Psalms: "I would rather be a doorkeeper in the House of God than to dwell in the tents of wickedness."

I also remembered a sermon by Augustine on "The Pure Love of God." He says in it something like this. To test whether you have the pure love of God, whether you obey God's first commandment, to love him above all else, imagine God himself approaching you and offering you everything in the world, everything you want. Nothing will be impossible to you, and nothing forbidden. Nothing is a sin, and nothing is punished. Whatever you imagine, you can have. There's only one catch—concluded God—you shall never, never see my face.

Augustine asks: Would you take that deal? If not, look what you've done. You've given up the whole world, and much more—all conceivable worlds—just for God. That is the pure (true) love of God.

I then knew why I had to choose to be last in heaven rather than first in hell, or earth, or even any paradise except heaven. I knew that to see his face, even as a mangy dog, is infinitely better than to rule all worlds and have all other goods.

I cried to God, "Let me be a dog; let me eat scraps; only let them be from your table!" And he smiled and opened heaven's gate to me.

I expected to be turned into a dog and be kicked. Instead, shining men and women crowded around me with congratulations. I asked them, "Wasn't I supposed to become a dog?" "Oh, yes," they said. "That's what you are. Right now. Just like us. You see, each of us was offered exactly the same choice as you: last in heaven or first in hell. And each of us chose what you chose. That's why we're here. Everyone gets what they choose. *Each* of us here is last, lowest, humblest. The Savior is the humblest of all. And each in hell is the highest, proudest, firstest. They're all prime ministers there."

I woke up, and the first thing that came to my mind was that "dog" is "God" spelled backwards. I thought that was God's little joke on us. Each of us is sort of God backwards, God imaged, God shadowed and reflected, infinity finitized. The thought of being a dog was not so shocking to me as the thought of sharing God's own life; for the difference between myself and a dog is nothing compared with the difference between myself and God!

If we are humble enough to accept who we are—God's dog, God's pets—we will be given table scraps from God's own table, God's own life. If we stand on our dignity and demand our rights, I fear that is exactly what we will get. Everyone in hell gets justice. Everyone in heaven gets bones and scraps of God, and even, perhaps, a high-spirited kick now and then. They can take that in heaven, because they can laugh at themselves there.

TWENTY-SEVEN

The Angel and the Ants

Once upon a time, in a universe long ago and far away, there was a wise and powerful spirit, an angel, who had an ant farm. His fellow angels couldn't understand what he saw in these dull, low, tiny creatures. But the angel loved his pet ants and spent enormous time, thought, and energy caring for them.

Then, one day, the ants decided to rebel against their angel caretaker. They announced, "We are mature ants now; we will not be under a caretaker any longer." When the angel warned them most solemnly against this, and reminded them of the simple fact that they were totally dependent on him, like it or not, they replied, "That is *your* truth. It is not *our* truth. We announce the subjectivity of truth."

So the ants erected a great shield under the glass of their ant farm so that they could no longer see their caretaker angel. Like ostriches hiding their heads in the sand, they thought this prevented *him* from seeing *them*. Of course, it did not. But they desperately wanted to protect themselves against the light that emanated from the angel's mind; for this light had become unbearably painful to them once they had rebelled, though before the rebellion it had been the source of all their joy and warmth.

Without the angel's light, the ants all shriveled up and died, one by one, in time. The angel was very sad, but he did not abandon his beloved ants. Instead, he set an invasion plan afoot. He made little laser cuts in the glass of the ant farm, and sent little shafts of light into the antennae of a few chosen ants, whom he made his prophets or mouthpieces. They were the advance guard of his planned invasion. These prophetic ants sternly reminded their brother and sister ants of the deathly consequences of continuing their rebellion. But few prophets were heeded, and most were killed, because even the tiny bits of reflected angel light the ants saw coming through the prophets' antennae caused the rebel ants unendurable pain and guilt.

Then came the master stroke of the angel's plan, the invasion. Though it seemed utterly mad, the angel, who had the power to materialize, became an ant himself. He was born from an obscure egg in a poor, out-of-the-way corner of the ant farm, and grew up as an ant among ants. All his angel prerogatives were left behind. He was fully ant even though he was angel. Many ants saw him as a great prophet, for his light miraculously healed thousands of ants dying of shrivelings in both body and mind. By his fellow ants he was wildly loved by some, wildly hated by others, and wildly misunderstood by all.

Finally, the inevitable happened: The ants all ran together at him and killed him to put out his light. But a tiny group of his followers were soon found going throughout the ant farm with a strange message. They seemed to be saying three very strange things about his body. First, they said this body rose from the dead. Second, they said they *were* his body. Thirdly, they said they *ate* his body. Few understood what this meant, and these strange sayings by themselves did not convince or convert many ants. But the love and joy and courage of his followers did, for it was like nothing any of the ants had ever seen before. So, many ants joined his band or his "body" and came to believe in the resurrection of his body. They claimed that the most precious thing in their lives was the continuing rite of eating his body. It seemed that the light of the angel, through the dead and risen body of his materialized prophet ant, had penetrated even the shield, like a spy, and come alive from within them. This they called his "spirit."

The angel-ant's enemies called this strange rite cannibalism and killed many of his followers, but they could not stop the movement. The more they fought it, the more it grew, until from one end of the ant farm to another, millions of ants were eating the dead and risen body of the angel-ant. And they claimed that one day soon the angel would destroy the shield entirely and come to take them home and live with them and make them angels forever.

A silly parable? Yes. Not really parallel to the story of Christianity? No. The criticism is absolutely correct, for a number of reasons.

First, the superiority of God over humanity is infinitely greater than that of an angel over an ant. For God is infinite, and the difference between infinity and any finitude is infinitely greater than the difference between any two finitudes. The distance the angel came, from his angel heaven, is infinitely less than the distance God came from his heaven. If the angel came from a mansion into a shack, God came from a throne into a mud puddle.

Second, the angel's rights over his ants were not absolute or total, for he was not the creator of their very being. And the ants' sin against their angel, bad as it was, was not *infinitely* horrible, for this reason. And the angel's act of saving them was not *infinitely* gratuitous, wild, and wonderful, utterly unpredictable and infinitely incredible—as was God's.

Third, Christ's intimacy with us in the Eucharist is far greater than the angel's intimacy with the ants. For the angel's love, however great, is not infinite, like God's. Therefore, the angel's sufferings, however great, could not be infinite, like God's. Also, the ant eucharist did not attain ontological union with God, with infinity, only with a finite creature, an angel.

No, the parable is not a very good one. But if it helps us to lift our eyes from this poor, weak story to the true one, which is infinitely richer and stronger, it may help humble us flat with wonder at what God really did. Then it will have served its only purpose.

TWENTY-EIGHT

How We Won the War: A Little Known Christmas Story

This is a true story. It took place on the eve of D-Day.

The greatest of world wars was at its most critical turning point. Until then, the war had been mostly a series of stunning victories for the Führer. Dictatorship had apparently proved highly efficient. Most of Western civilization was under his control. The world's only hope was the great counterattack, the invasion plans. Both sides suspected the time was ripe for D-day; the only unknowns were *when*, *where*, and *how*.

On the eve of the invasion, a conversation much like the following took place between two close friends, both captains in the invasion forces. The conversation was never written up in memoirs or reported in any newspaper—until now.

"Gabby, you know all about the invasion plans, don't you?"

"No, Mike. No one knows *all* about them. You know how Army Intelligence works."

"Sure, and also why. They're afraid you'd live up to your name and your gift of gab will get picked up by enemy ears."

"No way. Our new spy behind enemy lines has the only receiver that can pick up my messages. But I have to tell you some startling things tonight. The General himself told me to. It's you who have to keep this top secret."

"You know you can trust me, Gabby. I was only kidding about you."

"Captains don't kid, Mike. You know that. Now listen up. I have three secrets for you."

"Shoot."

"First, the invasion is tomorrow night."

"That's no surprise. What else?"

"The place. Look here on the map. It's a little town no one would ever suspect."

"There? Never heard of the place."

"After tomorrow, the whole world will know about it. We'll put it on the map."

"OK, what's the third secret?"

"The identity of our new spy. She's a woman."

"A woman! Why?"

"Mike, don't be such an old chauvinist. This one's perfect for the job, just perfect. She's been preparing the landing place now for months."

"How do you know all this?"

"I was the one that got the first message through. That was extremely tricky, let me tell you."

"Why?"

"Because I had to wait for her reply. Sending wireless messages is easy, but waiting to receive them is much harder. This one especially, because the General absolutely insisted that we wait until we got her permission."

"Permission? The General waited for the permission of a woman before the great invasion could happen?"

"Exactly."

"Why?"

"Well, he's a gentleman, you know. Very old-fashioned that way. And he knows the job is terribly dangerous."

"I'll bet. Look at what happened to all the spies we sent in before her."

"Yes. Most were tortured."

"So what if she had said no?"

"Then the whole invasion plan would have been scrapped, at least for now, maybe forever. Who knows?"

"Incredible! If I didn't know better, I'd swear the General had lost his marbles."

"You haven't heard the half of it. Hold on to your hat for this one, Mike. The General insisted on personally leading the invasion, not just directing it from across the Channel."

"What!"

"That's not all. He's already there, in disguise. He landed nine months ago."

"This is incredible, Gabby! And horribly dangerous. Suppose he's captured? What a plum *that* would be for the Führer! What kind of strategy is that—to walk right into the enemy's territory? Remember what happened to all those spies in the past? How does he expect to pull this off?"

"Well, the disguise is incredibly good, for one thing. But tomorrow, he's coming out of hiding. In fact, I think he may even be planning to be detected and eventually captured."

"What kind of a plan is that? Everything you tell me makes less and less sense than the thing before it. Why would he let himself be captured?"

"Believe it or not, I think he plans to confront the Führer himself, face to face."

"And what then?"

"I have no idea. He hasn't told anyone that."

"You know, if I didn't trust him implicitly...."

"I know. But you know what they say, 'Ours is not to reason why, ours is but to do or die.'"

"It's true, Gabby. That's the army way. Trust and obey."

"You know what I wonder about, Mike?"

"What?"

"Suppose the invasion works, and we liberate all the captive people. What will they do once they're freed? I'll bet many of them will still cling to the Führer's 'New Order.' It's so much a part of their lives now, it feels half comfortable to them—like a jail cell that's become your home. Even when you're paroled, you're afraid to leave. One thing is sure, anyway: Even if we win, the world will never be the same again: too many scars, too much devastation, no simple return to pre-war innocence."

"No, but we can at least give the tired old world a chance for a new start, eh?"

"Absolutely, Mike. By the way, who is 'we'? How many troops are in the invasion forces? If you're leading them tomorrow, you must know."

"You wouldn't believe it. The world has never seen an army this big. The whole sky is gonna have to open up for this one."

On Christmas Day, 4 B.C., the legions of General King of Kings under Michael the Archangel descended en masse in a field outside a little town called Bethlehem. The General himself came out of the hiding place Mary had prepared for him nine months before, disguised as a helpless baby.

The General wants all citizens to know that the invasion has been successful and the mop-up operation is still under way. All are urged to join this operation. There is still plenty to do. But the General assures all his troops that final, total victory is absolutely assured.

Hallmark is wrong. Christmas is not cute and cozy, sweet, and sentimental. Christmas is God's D-Day.

TWENTY-NINE

A Tale of Dragons

Once upon a time there was a great King, who ruled over many different kingdoms. One of them was the Kingdom of Dragons.

All the dragons were originally good dragons. But the King of the Dragons, jealous that he could not be the equal of the great King, rebelled against the great King and persuaded many of the other dragons to join his rebellion.

The great King expelled the Dragon-King and his allies from the dragon kingdom, but the Dragon-King had such strong magic that he was able to sneak into another of the many kingdoms which the great King ruled. This other kingdom was called the Kingdom of Animals. The Kingdom of Animals was ruled by the King and Queen of the Animals. They were the rulers because they were the only animals that could talk, think, and make decisions.

Now the Dragon-King used his strong magic to disguise himself as a worm, and he crept into an apple in the castle garden of the King and Queen of the Animals. The great King, who knew all that happened in all of his many kingdoms, knew this too, and warned the King and Queen of the Animals not to eat that particular apple. He knew that if they did, they would swallow the Dragon-Worm; and once he was inside them, they would die. He also knew that if all this happened, then the strong magic of the Dragon-King would make him able to turn back into a dragon and kill all the other talking animals with his fire-breath.

So the great King warned the King and Queen of the Animals not to eat that particular apple. But just because he had picked out that particular apple, they were curious, and fascinated, and began to wonder what would really happen if they ate it. So they did. And everything the great King had warned them against came true.

Now the Kingdom of the Animals was in a sad state. All the other animals began to fight and kill each other, because the King and the Queen were no longer able to rule and tame them, since they were now terribly sick from the poison worm in the apple they had eaten. Furthermore, the Dragon-King had turned back into a full-sized dragon and was now threatening to kill every single talking animal in the kingdom with his fiery breath. No shield could stop that fire, and no hiding place, not even underground, could keep the talking animals safe from it. It seemed that there was nothing anyone could do, not even the great King himself, to save the poor talking animals from the Dragon-King.

But the great King had a son as wise as he. Every decision he made, they made together. Now the son came to his father and said, "Father, there is a way to save this kingdom of yours, and I would like to volunteer to do the job. They have unleashed the dragon and his fiery breath upon their land, and that cannot be undone. And none of them can stand up to that breath. But I can. Let me go out into this kingdom and entice the dragon to come after me. He will see me in his own land and think he can kill me with his breath. He will expend all his hate and fire on me, so there will be none left in him to kill the other talking animals."

The great King said to his son: "But the fire will hurt you terribly, my son. All the hate-fire that the dragon had for all the many talking animals in the kingdom, he will concentrate on you. You will feel all the fire in the world, and you will be burned and die."

"Yes, Father, but I have a stronger magic than his. After I die, I will come to life again, and tie the dragon up with strong ropes. Now, his fire can reach throughout the kingdom. If I fool him so that he spits all his hate-fire at me, he will have only tiny bits left, and he will be able to harm only those foolish enough to wander close to him. For I will tie him on a short leash."

The plan was exactly what the great King had thought up, too, and he was glad that his son had exactly the same thought. So the King said "Go, my son," although with a sad heart, for he knew how much the dragon's fire would hurt his dear son. The King's heart suffered even more than the son when the dragon attacked him with his fire-breath, for love always multiplies sorrows as well as joys.

But they carried through with their plan. When the Dragon-King saw the great King's son coming into his kingdom, he thought the King had gone soft in the head. "I could not touch him or reach him while he was safe in his palace," the dragon thought, "but now he has stepped right into my trap."

And he hunted down the King's son for years. When he finally found him, he poured all of his hate and all of his fire on him and burned him to a crisp. The dragon's laughter at this point was the most horrible sound ever heard, in that kingdom or in any other. But just as he had planned, the Prince came to life again, and bound the dragon. And thus, all the talking animals in the kingdom were saved, except those foolish enough to visit the tied-up dragon and venture close enough to him to be burned by the little bit of fire-breath he had left.

PART SIX

Suffering

THIRTY

Some Common Christian Sense about Suffering

Suffering is the best reason in the world for losing or abandoning the faith, but it is also the best reason in the world for keeping it.

The reason is all around us, especially in this century, "the devil's century," as the vision of Pope Leo XIII called it, the century which has seen our society slide farther and farther down the social garbage drain, taking individuals and families with it to multitudinous and accelerating disasters: divorce, drugs, sodomy, AIDS, infidelity (both sexual and ecclesiastical), violence, homelessness, defeminization, demasculinization, you name it. Just to quote one statistic: Teenage violent crimes are up 5,000 percent since the fifties.

"If there is a God, why are these terrible things happening?"

This is the most frequently heard reason for abandoning the faith, especially when "these terrible things," which we always knew were happening, affect us personally, through our own friends, families, or selves. The problem is as old as Job. Only the forms are new. We always knew this was a "vale of tears," we just conveniently forgot it for a while, surrounded as we were with technological securities and progressivist, optimistic ideologies.

Life has terrible things in store for all of us: "premature" deaths, crippling accidents, betrayals, suicides, alcoholism, abortions, or perhaps just cold, controlled lovelessness, the greatest tragedy of all—imperviousness to tragedy.

In this world, it is guaranteed that everyone's heart will be broken somehow. In light of that fact, there are two opposite ways of looking at the faith.

One can look at it as theory or practice; abstractly, or concretely; as a blueprint, or as a life preserver. If you think of faith as a blueprint, a theory, then the terrible things that happen do not seem to fit neatly into the theory. They are like an extra piece in a jigsaw puzzle. Even though the theory, the doctrines of Christianity, include the proviso that "in this world you will have tribulation," even though we are assured of this by Christ himself repeatedly, yet it is hard for us to really believe this sometimes, hard to let it sink in. If the all-powerful God, who has the whole world in his hands, is good, and loving, and kind, how could he let things go so terribly, terribly wrong? Perhaps the doctrine is not true after all. The *experience* certainly is—the experience of real evil—and doctrine must be tested by experience, mustn't it, as scientific theory must be tested by relevant data?

Instead of answering this classic problem of evil on its own ground, which is theoretical, I think it is better to shift the ground first before answering it. Not only because this book is about religion, not theology; relationship with God, not theory about God. But also because this is the most helpful way of looking at the Christian faith: as a practical life preserver. Jesus was not a professor but a Savior. He came fundamentally not to preach but to die. God gave us his Word, the Bible, just as he gave us his Word, Jesus Christ, not as a puzzle for scholars but as an ark for sailors.

Oh, we could answer the problem on the theoretical level. We could point out that the experience of the power of evil does not contradict the Christian teaching, but it contradicts another teaching: a Pollyanna religion, derived not from the Bible or the church but from pop psychology or human expectations; a religion with a heaven but no hell, a real good but no real evil, a creation but no fall, a sermon on the mount but no Calvary.

But it is a stronger answer to say that the faith is not a hypothesis at all. It is more like a crutch. People used to accuse religion of being a crutch. The answer is: Yes. That's exactly what it is. What is more necessary for a cripple than a crutch? And if you don't think you are a cripple, you must have been on a long vacation from the real world for the last few decades.

Walker Percy, asked why he became a Catholic, replied: "What else is there?" G.K. Chesterton replied, to the same question: "To get my sins forgiven." Once we realize that we are drowning, we do not complain if the only ark of salvation has a lot of smells from the animal stalls. There are few atheists on deathbeds, and those few are life's true fools.

When you are dying, the faith reveals its true beauty and power, and even its truth. What do you tell the dying if all you believe in is "peace and justice," or "brotherhood," or "caring and sharing?" What does modern wisdom say to the dying? "Have a nice day"? What does the pop psychologist say to the dying? "I'm OK, you're OK"? What does the liberal theologian say to the dying? "Be up to date"?

It is well known that "the blood of the martyrs is the seed of the church," that the church has always thrived under persecution and languished under prosperity. That is why she is far stronger in the Third World than in the First; in China and Africa and Lithuania than in England and America and Sweden and Holland. The same is true of individuals. We realize how strong is the power of the cross to save only when we realize how strong is the power of the cross to make us suffer.

If you are suffering right now, know that this fits in perfectly with what God predicted, with his perfect plan to sculpt your soul and save your world. Don't let this puzzle you, or surprise you.

Here is what the first pope said to you: "Beloved, do not be surprised at the fiery ordeal which comes upon you to prove you, as though something strange were happening to you. But rejoice in so far as you share Christ's sufferings, that you may also rejoice and be glad when his glory is revealed" (1 Pt 4:12-13). Suffering is an investment in the bank of eternal joy.

If you are not suffering right now, remember and pray regularly for those who are, especially those you know by name. For "more things are wrought by prayer than this world dreams of." The martyrs' strength was supported by the faithful's prayers. And when it comes your turn, those prayers will support you, too.

THIRTY-ONE

When God Says No

Lord, he whom you love is ill. **John 11:3**

We come to him with the same needs and perhaps even the same words as Martha when her beloved brother Lazarus was ill. We believe the situation is not fundamentally changed; that he is "the same yesterday, today, and forever" (Heb 13:8), that he can heal now as he healed then, both by miracle and by providential control of the forces of nature. We also know that he loves us, knows us, cares for us—that we are like Lazarus, as beloved to him as our own kin is to us. We also know that he has explicitly told us to beseige heaven with our prayers, like the neighbor in the night (Lk 11:5-10) or the widow who kept pestering the unjust judge (Lk 18:1-8). Finally, we know that he has promised us that "all who ask, receive" (Mt 7:7-8; Mk 11:24; Jn 15:7; 16:23).

How then are we to understand it when, despite our faith, our hope, our love, and our prayers, a dear one dies? Especially when the death seems so pointless, for instance, the death of a child? Of course, we all must die, but some deaths seem "clean deaths"—just, right, ready, proper—while others seem "dirty deaths"—deaths that raise clouds of doubt like dust into the eyes of faith.

A woman approached me after Mass once, choking back the tears. She wanted to know about my daughter's nearly miraculous recovery from a brain tumor some years ago because her own daughter, now twenty-two, had just been told by the doctors that she had a malignant brain tumor.

What could I say? My daughter had been one of the "lucky" ones. Hers might not be. God's answer to my prayers had been yes, and this woman wanted some assurance from me that God's answer to her prayers would be yes, too. But I could not give her that assurance. I had no word of prophecy, no way of knowing whether or even why God would give her her hoped for answer. The doctors had given her very "bad odds." But (as she already knew) it's Doctor God who sets the "odds." They had given my daughter very bad odds, too. The calculation of odds, which at first seems so crucially important to us when we first hear devastating news like that, drops away into insignificance at some stage in our spiritual growth (a growth that can accelerate with alarming swiftness when a bombshell like a brain tumor suddenly explodes in our comfortable foxhole). We realize soon that with God there are no odds at all. With God everything is certain. "Man proposes, God disposes."

But was I to tell that little philosophy lesson to this distraught woman? Philosophy is weaker than tears. I remembered only too well how I had learned that. I remembered my own panic at the sudden prospect of facing my daughter's slow, agonizing dying. My *faith* did not fall apart when the doctors delivered the sentence—six to twelve months to live—but *I* did. I thought, God made a mistake! I'm not up to this. I'm a pampered softie, not a tough saint. It turned out (as it always does, and as we sometimes see) that God made no mistake. He tempered the wind to the shorn lamb.

What could I give this woman, if not my "specialty," philosophy? Only what we all can give, the most precious thing: prayer, which contains faith, hope, and love, the three most precious things in the world. They can be invested in others' accounts by intercessory prayer. My own daughter was saved, I am convinced, only because hundreds of people prayed for her. I know I am a poor pray-er, but even my tenth-rate prayers can be twenty times more useful and powerful for her than my second-rate philosophizing. One drop of blood from a heart that really bleeds for another can heal more than the pale diagrams of thought.

I remembered asking God the question she must now be asking him a thousand times, the question millions ask. After we do our part, after we pray and believe and hope and love, God seems not to hear. If he hears (and we know he does; faith assures us of that), he refuses. He answers, but his answer is no. The question then is: Why? Why me, Lord? What good can this death possibly do? What life is fertilized by this death? And is it really necessary for God to use such expensive fertilizer? (I choose an image that sounds shockingly unfeeling because death seems shockingly unfeeling.) No human father with an ounce of compassion could stand stoically by and allow a travesty of justice and charity like the death of a young mother and the devastation of her family to go on without acting against it. Why does our heavenly Father seem to do exactly that?

Here is the answer. Sometimes the hardest things to notice are the things up so close that they're like the nose in front of our face. The obviously true answer to the question, "Why?"—that great question, that agonizing question, that needy, desperately needy question—is very clear. It's the message of Job, perhaps the most profound and most philosophical book in the Bible. Yet many scholars and philosophers miss it—*most*, in fact (though not my favorite philosopher, Socrates). Only the simple, only the childlike, only the humble, get it. The embarrassingly obvious answer is: We don't know.

The question is not the general question of the problem of evil, or the problem of suffering. The question is not: Why do bad things ever happen to good people? But: Why is this bad thing happening to this good person? General answers—which we have—are not specific answers—which we don't have.

Might God be letting these trials happen to test our faith? Yes, but God knows everything. He doesn't need to perform any experiments to test and find anything out. Nothing is unknown to him. Might God do it then not for his sake but for our sakes, to strengthen our faith, like gold tested in the fire? Certainly, that is true. Scripture says so. But our faith is not always strengthened by fire. Sometimes it's weakened. Sometimes it breaks. We don't always pass the test. Sometimes we fail, fall apart, lose hope, withdraw, give up, even flail out in resentment and rebellion. We see concentration camps make saints out of some, but animals or zombies out of others. Why does God allow us to be buffeted so badly that we go under? Why doesn't he always temper the wind to the shorn lamb?

We can speculate and guess, of course. We can extrapolate from what we know to what we don't know. But the absolutely necessary first answer, if we are honest, is that we ***don't*** know, anymore than Eve knew why that one fruit was forbidden. If we knew, we wouldn't need faith, only sight and reason.

Why is it so hard for us to admit or even to notice the blindingly obvious truth that we don't know the answer to this awful question? Because we desperately want to latch onto some answer, some sense, some meaning that we can understand. Our thirst for understanding is natural and good. But sometimes we die of thirst. It is no good pretending that sand is wine.

Faced with a woman's tears of thirst, I remembered my own time of thirst, of ignorance. It was a time of grace, too, because it was a time not just of ignorance but also of knowledge: of the knowledge, precisely, of my ignorance—lesson one. On no other foundation can we erect any lesson two. Just as saints recognize they are sinners, and sinners deny it, so the wise recognize they are fools, and fools deny it.

We never grow up. "Adult" is a word used only by fools, pop psychologists, and pornographers. There ***are*** no adults. (As for "adult" pornography, why is their bible called *Playboy Magazine*?) There are biological adults, of course. But there are no spiritual adults. Anyone who claims he is spiritually mature is a fool, that is, a spiritual infant. And anyone who claims he is *not* spiritually mature is telling the truth, that is, he *is* a spiritual infant. Either way, we are all spiritual infants. Thou shalt not pretend to be adult; thou shalt not commit adult-ery.

Our highest relationship with God is the relationship God had with God. What did incarnate God call unincarnate God? Not just "Father" but "Abba," "Da-da"—baby talk.

What did the greatest theologian of all time, a saint and Doctor of the Church, call his masterpiece, the greatest work of theology of all time? St. Thomas Aquinas called the *Summa Theologiae* "straw," and refused to write another word after he had seen God, in mystical experience, by infused contemplation, by supernatural gift. If the clear, brightly burning words of St. Thomas are straw, ours are spiderwebs, gossamer, fog, dust in the wind. (But if the wind is the wind of the Spirit, even our specks of dust can work the work of God, *opus dei*.)

We don't know why our prayers for healing are not answered. I honestly believe our gentle heavenly Father is very, very angry at his self-appointed defenders who claim from pulpit or TV screen to know what no one knows, especially the ones who cause many of the little ones for whom Christ died to stumble and despair by the horrible "gospel" of prosperity, health, and healing that they preach. They say God wants us well and that all we have to do is to have faith. So if we don't get well, if healing doesn't happen, if prayers are refused, it's because we have failed. We have not had enough faith. What a horrible crime: to lay on the sorrowing head of God's little ones weeping for their beloved dead the additional unbearable burden of guilt! If it's true that "if only I had had more faith, my dear one would not have died," then I am to blame for his death!

Perhaps these preachers' motive is good: to get God off the hook. Don't blame God. No, but don't blame us either. Blame the devil. Restoration of faith in the devil's real existence is crucially important for psychological health. Without him to blame, you either blame no one and become a wimp or a stoic, or you blame yourself and become a guilt-ridden neurotic, or you blame God and hate him.

The reason I dare to suppose God is very angry at this is because his meek and gentle Son said some shockingly terrifying things about those who cause one of his little ones to stumble—something about millstones.

Is that all, then? We don't know why God says no, but we know we don't know, and that we must admit it? Is that all?

That depends. We cannot go on down this road of understanding why *unless* God opens it, as he did when the disciples asked him why the man had been born blind. They had two neat explanations: Was it punishment for his sins or for his parents'? They gave the Lord a multiple choice test. But the Lord does not *take* our multiple choice tests. He *gives* them. He does not fit our options, we fit his.

Christ's answer was, as usual, not usual. Neither this man's sin nor his parents' was the reason. He was born blind—God had allowed this tragedy—so that the glory of God could appear through him: That is, so that Jesus could work this miracle of healing. Note the surprise: not just the miracle, but that the illness was for the miracle, not the miracle for the illness. His healing was a means to the end of Christ's work of bringing and showing the kingdom, not vice versa. Jesus is not just a doctor, even a miracle-working doctor, or a social worker, or a psychiatrist. Jesus is Lord, alpha and omega, beginning and end of all things, including this man and his life and his blindness.

In this one, Jesus lifted the curtain of our ignorance a little. He explained the connection. In most cases he does not do that, and we are stuck with faith, not sight: "Thomas, because you have seen, you have believed. Blessed are those who have not seen and yet have believed."

We usually have the world inside out: We call ourselves *I*, the center, and God *thou*, the other. But God is *I*, the center. His essential name is "I am." For him and from him everything else takes its meaning. Everything in the world is a ray of light from the Sun of God. Suffering and death too, and therefore God's policy of nonintervention, God's nonhealing, God's awful no to our prayers, are also *for this end.* "*All* things work together for good."

But what does this mean? These things are not *for* him in the sense that he needs them, surely. And they do not seem to be *for* him but against him in the great battle between good and evil, for when he was on earth he showed himself the enemy of diseases by healing, and the enemy of death by rising from the dead. He did not accept these things like a stoic or a Hindu; he fought them. How then can we say that these things—sickness, suffering, and death—are *for* him?

In that they effect his will, his kingdom, his glory. What is his will? Love. What is his kingdom? The kingdom of love. What is his glory? Nothing but the glory of love. He does all that he does because he loves us. He answers no because he loves. Out of love he heals and out of love he refuses to heal. His no is as much the word of love as his yes. In one way his no is *more* the word of love than his yes. Did he not love his own Son infinitely? Yet look at the no Christ got in Gethsemane and on the cross.

"Father, if it be possible, take this cup from me."

"No."

"My God, my God, why hast thou forsaken me?"

No answer. God himself asked our agonizing question on the cross and, like us, got no answer. When we ask and agonize, we are nearest to his heart.

It was all part of his incredibly gracious plan: He shared our forsakenness, our not getting an answer, so that we could share his, so that our not getting an answer from the Father could be the most intimate, Christlike experience. We are never closer to Christ than when we suffer with him. That is his work, the work he came to earth for: not primarily to teach or even to heal but to suffer and die. And he has graciously allowed us to join him in his high and holy work. He has somehow joined our sufferings to his by joining us to him in his body. *That* is his universal solution to suffering; healings are his occasional particular solutions. He has joined some of our sufferings to his glory by healing them, but he has joined all our sufferings to his humiliation, by suffering them.

That means that our sufferings now have power. They *work*. They have the power of the cross, the power to help save souls, soften hearts, and change the world more radically than any conqueror can. Nothing offered to God is ever wasted. "What a waste!" we say of a life cut short, a twenty-two-year-old woman dying of a brain tumor. No. We are wrong. We see little. That is not a waste. That is the cross. The cross is not a waste. Nothing was ever less a waste than the cross.

When Christ walked our earth, he performed miracles not to solve the problem of suffering but to manifest the kingdom of God. As a solution to suffering, his healings were woefully inadequate. How many lepers were there in Israel? And of them, how many did he heal? Modern medicine could have healed more! Jesus barely scratched the surface of earth's miseries. He could have cleaned up all the dirt in the world by his omnipotent word of miracle-working power—and still can—but he didn't. And what he didn't do is as instructive as what he did do. He did not take away St. Paul's "thorn in the flesh." He did not take away suffering from the saints. Indeed, one of them said, "The cross is the gift God gives to his friends." His *friends*! His own Son, his friends, the saints—these, not outcasts and enemies, are refused.

We do not know *how* it works, how suffering redeems. But we know *that* it works. We do not know *why* this has to be his policy, but we know *that* it is. And we know *who* he is who sets this policy: omniscient and omnipotent love. All-seeing love says "no" to little-seeing "please." Daddy says no to baby. Why? Because Daddy doesn't love baby? Oh, no. Love can say no as well as yes, and baby doesn't usually understand. But baby can trust—unless baby insists on being an adult.

"Though he slay me, yet will I trust in him," says Job (Jb

13:15, KJV). Most of us cannot honestly lay claim to that kind of faith, I think, and I suspect that if we seem to ourselves to find it easy to repeat these words, we are playing games with God and with ourselves. It's perilously easy to imagine ourselves playing saint, to confuse the dream with the actuality, the wish with the will. Do we really want to be Job? Do we really love the old rugged cross on our own backs? We love to sing about it and contemplate it from a distance, but bearing it is, frankly, a dirty, ugly job.

Until, like Simon of Cyrene, we see him bearing it alone, and rush in love to help. Until we see him in his children, in "the poorest of the poor," and rush in, not with a moralist's calculation but with a mother's spontaneous love, or a friend's. Then we bear the cross as he did: for love.

Nothing elicits love like suffering. If there were no more suffering in the world, if science eliminated suffering, there would be no more love. Overcoming lovelessness is infinitely more important than overcoming suffering. To suffer and to love is profoundly meaningful; not to suffer *and not to love* is an intolerable "brave new world" of meaningless boredom. God allows suffering for the sake of love. Ideally, we should be able to love without suffering, but this is not Eden or heaven where that was and will be possible. Here, suffering is the price of loving; the cross is the price of salvation.

Every one of us gets one big no from God: death. And we know why: that no is the means to the greatest yes, heaven. "Thou hast made death glorious and triumphant, for through its portals we enter into the presence of the living God," says an oratorio. But the little nos, the little deaths, are also means to the end of yes. They are God cracking the egg of our lives (ouch!) so that the bird can fly out, or crawl out—one day he will fly. "He will bear you up on eagle's wings."

Again, we do not know *how* this works, or even *why* it works, but we know *that* it works, because God's Word tells us so.

"So we do not lose heart. Though our outer nature is wasting away, our inner nature is being renewed every day. For this slight momentary affliction is preparing for us an eternal weight of glory beyond all comparison, because we look not to the things that are seen but to the things that are unseen; for the things that are seen are transient but the things that are unseen are eternal." **2 Corinthians 4:16-18**

THIRTY-TWO

How Does the Weakness of the Cross Make Us Strong?

"When I am weak, then I am strong"; "power made perfect in weakness." Such verses are often cited as key to spiritual growth, but do we really understand what they are talking about? Can anyone ever understand?

Yes. If we couldn't understand it at all, God would not have told it to us. God does not waste words. It is a great mystery, but a mystery is not something we cannot understand at all, but something we cannot understand by our own reason, without God's revelation. It is also something we cannot understand wholly, but something we can understand partly. Partial understanding is not total darkness. "We see through a glass, darkly."

The key to the mystery of strength made perfect in weakness is the cross of Christ. Without the cross it is not a mystery but an absurdity, a darkness.

But non-Christians like the great Chinese mystic and poet Lao Tzo seem to have understood the mystery of strength made perfect in weakness quite profoundly, at least in some of its aspects, without knowing Christ or the cross.

Perhaps they understand a similar and related mystery but not quite the same one. Or perhaps they understand it through Christ and his cross too, though not consciously and explicitly. How do we know where the boundaries of the cross extend to? Its arms are very wide. Christ is "the light that enlightens every man who comes into the world" (Jn 1:9) by natural revelation, natural wisdom, and the natural law known by conscience. When a Lao Tzo, or a Socrates, or a Buddha arrive at a profound knowledge of some eternal truth, they do so by the light of Christ, the eternal Logos, the pre-incarnate Word or revelation of God. He is the same ***person***, but not with his human, incarnate ***nature***. All truth is his truth.

But the ***incarnate*** Jesus is God's definitive revelation, God's face turned to us in utmost intimacy. We know far more of a person through his face than his back or his feet. So let's look at that final, definitive, total revelation of God that we have—Christ and his cross—to try to shed some light on our paradox of strength coming from weakness. Our question is: How does weakness make us strong through the cross? Or, how does the weakness of the cross make us strong?

There are two questions here, not one. The first is theoretical and unanswerable. The second is practical and answerable.

The first question is: How does it work? By what supernatural, spiritual technology does the machine of weakness produce the product of strength? How does the cross work?

Theologians have been working on that one for nearly two thousand years, and there is no clear consensus in Christendom, no obviously adequate answer, only analogies. St. Anselm's legal analogy is of the devil owning us and Christ paying the price to buy us back. The early Church Fathers gave a cosmic battle analogy: Christ invaded enemy-occupied territory—first earth, then, on Holy Saturday, the underworld, and defeated the devil and his forces of sin and death. Then there is the Southern Free-Will Baptist preacher's delightfully simple Americanism: "Satan votes agin' ye, an' Jesus votes for ye, and ye cast the deciding vote." These metaphors are helpful, but they are only symbols, likenesses. We hardly know how electricity works; how can we know how redemption works?

A second question, however, is more definitely answerable. That is the practical question: How should I live; how should I behave in relation to weakness? How should I enact the cross in my life? For the cross is in my life. It is not a freak but a universal truth incarnated, not merely a once-for-all event outside me in space and time, in Israel in A.D. 29, separated from me by eight thousand miles and two thousand years, but also a continuing event within me, or rather I within it.

There are two equal and opposite errors in answering the question: How shall I enact this mystery of the cross in my life? They are humanism and quietism, activism and passivism. Humanism says that all is human action, that we must fight and overcome weakness, failure, defeat, disease, death, and suffering. We must overcome the cross. But we never do, in the end. Humanism is Don Quixote riding forth on a horse to fight a tank.

Quietism, or fatalism, says simply: Endure it, accept it. In other words, don't be human. *Go* "gentle into that good night," do ***not*** "rage, rage against the dying of the light."

Christianity is more paradoxical than the simple no of humanism or the simple yes of fatalism. There is the same paradoxical doubleness in the Christian answer to poverty, suffering, and death. Poverty is to be fought against and relieved, yet it is blessed. Helping the poor to escape the ravages of their poverty is one of the essential Christian duties. If we refuse it, we are not Christians, we are not saved (Mt 25:41-46). Yet it is the rich who are pitied and pitiable, as Mother Teresa so startlingly told Harvard: "Don't call my country a poor country. India is not a poor country. America is a poor country, a spiritually poor country." It is very hard for a rich man to be saved (Mt 19:23), while the poor in spirit, that is, those willing to be poor, those detached from riches, are blessed (Mt 5:3).

The same paradoxical double attitude is found in Christianity toward death. Death is on the one hand the great evil, the "last enemy" (1 Cor 15:26), the mark and punishment of sin. Christ came to conquer it. Yet death is also the door to eternal life, to heaven. It is the golden chariot sent by the great king to fetch his Cinderella bride.

Suffering is a paradox too. On the one hand, it is to be relieved, on the other hand it is blessed. The saints are saints mainly for two reasons: they have heroic love and compassion for their neighbors, that is, they give their all to *relieve* others' sufferings. But they also love God so much that they *accept* and offer up their own sufferings heroically and even joyfully. They both fight and accept suffering. They are more active than humanists and more accepting than quietists.

All three—poverty, death, and suffering—are forms of weakness. The problem of weakness is the more general, universal problem. Suffering, for instance, is not in itself as intolerable as weakness, for we willingly embrace pains like childbirth if only they are freely chosen, in our power—but even small pains and inconveniences, like late planes or stubbed toes, we find outrageous and intolerable if they are imposed on us against our will. We would rather run a mile freely than be forced to run a block. Kierkegaard says, "If I had a humble servant who, when I asked him for a glass of water, brought instead the world's costliest wines perfectly blended in a chalice, I would fire him, to teach him that true pleasure consists in getting my own way."

Freud's maverick disciple Alfred Adler parted company with his teacher on the central issue of what the most basic human desire is; it is not pleasure, as Freud thought, but power, Adler discovered.

Even St. Thomas Aquinas implicitly agrees, for when he reviews and eliminates all the idolatrous and inadequate candidates for the position of supreme human happiness, all the things we pursue instead of God, he notes that we are attracted to power because it seems most godly. (This, however, is deceptive because God's power *is* his goodness.)

Power is St. Augustine's answer to why he stole hard, inedible, and unsellable pears as a boy. He wanted not pleasure or money but power—the power not to be under a law of "thou shalt not steal," the power to disobey the law and apparently get away with it. We rankle under restraint.

Ah, but our very being is restraint. We are, after all, only creatures, not the creator; finite through and through, not infinite; mortal, not immortal; ignorant, not all-knowing. All these are forms of weakness, and not accidental and avoidable weaknesses, but weaknesses innate and essential to our very being as creatures. In resenting the restrictions of weakness we resent our own being.

Before we even begin to try to get *out* of our problem of strength out of weakness, we must first look more deeply and clearly *into* it. There are three related but distinct weaknesses to look at.

First, there is the weakness of being second, playing second fiddle, responding rather than initiating, following rather than leading, obeying rather than commanding. Our resentment against this is totally foolish, for God himself includes this weakness! From all eternity the Son obeys the Father. What he did on earth, he did in eternity. "He did, in the wild weather of his outlying provinces, what he had done eternally in home in glory," as George MacDonald put it. No one was ever more obedient than Christ.

Therefore, obedience is not a mark of inferiority. To respond, to sing second voice, to play second fiddle, is not demeaning, for the Christ who is very God of very God, was the perfect obeyer. In this we have one of the most astounding and radical revolutions the world has ever heard, and has not yet understood. Women still resent being women, that is, biologically receptive to male impregnation and needing male protection and leadership, because they think this makes them inferior. Children resent having to obey parents, and citizens resent having to obey civil authority, for the same reason: They think this obedience marks their inferiority. It does not.

Christ was and is equal to the Father in all things; yet Christ obeyed and is even now obeying the Father. Difference in role does not mean difference in worth. The "weakness" of obedience comes not from inferiority but from equality in value.

Children are also to obey parents. Yet children are not the moral or spiritual inferiors of parents. The command to obey does not demean but liberates—*if* we are talking about the obedience "in Christ." In the world, power rules, and the strong impose themselves on the weak. There, obedience is indeed a mark of inferiority in power. But not in the church. Here, everything is different: "You know that the rulers of the gentiles lord it over them, and their great men exercise authority over them. It shall not be so among you; but whoever would be great among you must be your servant, and whoever would be first among you must be your slave; even as the Son of Man came not to be served but to serve, and to give his life as a ransom for many" (Mt 20:25-28).

Jesus was equal to the Father, yet obeyed. If that simple but revolutionary fact were understood and appreciated, we would have a new world—not the ancient world of slavery and oppression, nor the modern Western world of uprootedness and disorder, of unnatural levelling and resentful competition. We would have instead *love.*

Love makes strength. The "weakness" of Christ in obeying the Father made him strong because it was the obedience of love. Had Christ disobeyed the Father's will, as Satan tempted him to do in the wilderness, he would have lost his strength, as Samson did, and weakly succumbed to his enemy. His obedience was a mark of his divinity. And we too: If we obey the Father completely, we are transformed into participants in the divine nature. For repentance, faith, and baptism, the three instruments of that transformation, are all forms of obedience. We are *commanded* to repent, believe, and be baptized.

A second form of "weakness" is proper only to us, not to Christ, but this second form, too, is not to be resented. It is our finitude, our creatureliness. We were created. We are therefore dependent on God for everything, for our very existence and all that flows from it. Nothing we have is our own because our very being is not our own. God owns us. (Suicide is therefore theft.) We have no rights over against God. No creature does, not even the greatest archangel.

No creature is omnipotent, nor is any creature totally impotent. Even an angel cannot create a universe or save a soul; but even a grain of sand can manifest God, can irritate a toe and a mind, and can decide a battle and a war.

Not even in eternity will any creature exhaust God and finish the exploration into his love. God will always be *more.* We will never lose the incomparable pleasure of humility, of hero-worship. How silly to resent that "weakness."

And how silly to resent God's and nature's compensation for that weakness, namely mutual interdependence, solidarity, cooperation, unselfishness. We bear each other's burdens, thereby fulfilling the law of Christ (Gal 6:2). I think the phrase "law of Christ" means more than just obeying Christ's commands; I think it means living Christ's life. I think the law of Christ is like the law of gravity rather than like the law of the land here. Falling apples fulfill the law of gravity, and bearing one another's burdens fulfills the law of Christ.

Marriage is the prime example of bearing each other's burdens. Men need women, as God observed at creation: "It is not good for man to be alone" (Gn 2:18). And women need men. Both often resent that need today. That is rebellion against the law of Christ, which is inscribed in the law of human nature. The very image of God is identified in Genesis 1:27 as "male and female."

Finally, there is a third form of weakness, which it is right to rail against: the weakness of sin and its effects. It is good to be finite, but not to be fallen. We are all abnormal, not in our natural state. We do well here to rebel against what we are, for what we are is not natural, not what God designed. Our dissatisfaction with our moral and spiritual weakness implicitly testifies to our knowledge of something better—of a standard by which we measure ourselves, our lives, and our world, and find them wanting. It is our memory of Eden that causes our present lover's quarrel with the world, with this wilderness "east of Eden" (Gn 3:24).

It is because we are morally weak that we are commanded to pray "lead us not into temptation," that is, into trials and difficulties. For we all have our breaking point. Unless God had shortened the days of the Great Tribulation, even the saints would not endure and be saved (Mt 24:22).

We are not only morally weak but also intellectually weak: ignorant, foolish, stupid. Sin is not *mere* foolishness as Plato taught, and certainly its cause is not only ignorance as Plato taught, but while ignorance is not the *cause* of sin, it *is* the *effect* of sin.

Also our body is weak because of sin. Once the soul declared independence from God, the source of all life and power, the body became weak because it became more independent from the soul, the source of its life. Death is thus a necessary result of sin. It is like a magnet. God is the magnet that holds two iron rings, body and soul, together. Take away the magnet, and the rings fall apart. Once we are apart from God, what should we do but die? And once we are with God, what should we do but live forever?

We should accept obedience to the Father as our first "weakness," and we should accept being finite as our second "weakness," but should we also accept our third "weakness," our sinfulness? Yes and no. Sin is like cancer. When we have cancer, we should accept that fact with our intellect but not with our will. We should accept the truth, but not the goodness of the cancer, because cancer is *not* good. Accept it theoretically, but not practically. On the practical level we should fight it. The same is true of sin.

People are often confused about this simple point. Even a great mind like Carl Jung seems to descend into this deadly confusion when he tells us to "accept our own dark side, our shadow." No! God had to die and suffer the horrors of hell to save us from that dark side. How dare we "accept" it when the Holy One has declared eternal war against it? How dare we be neutral when God takes sides? How dare we play Chamberlain at Munich to the inventions of hell? Only one fate is proper for such spiritual wimpiness. Look it up in Revelation 3:16. What God has vomited up, let no one try to eat.

I now venture into deeper, more perilous areas of our problem.

Our weakness becomes our strength when God enters into our weakness. Like a doctor anesthetizing a patient so that he ceases to be an agent and becomes a patient, becomes passive, so that he does not hop about on the operating table, God weakens us so that he can perform operations on us that would otherwise be impossible.

This is especially true of death. Death is radical surgery, and we must be radically anesthetized for it. God wants to penetrate into our heart, our innermost being. Our heart must stop beating for that operation to take place.

The same principle works in lesser ways before death, in little deaths. God has to knock us out first in order to rescue us from drowning, for we flail about foolishly. He has to slap our hands empty of our toys to fill them with his joys.

So far, so good. That principle is fairly well known. But when we turn to the mystics and read their strange language about "becoming nothing," the consummation of weakness, we shake our heads in incomprehension and suspicion. Yet the mystics' sense of "nothingness" before God is nothing but the same principle taken to its logical conclusion. If God's strength fills us when we are weak, and God's greatness fills us when we are little, then God's all fills us when we are nothing.

But we must distinguish between two kinds of "nothing." Oriental mystics seem to say that the soul is "nothing" because it is not real. They see through the "illusion" of individuality. They seem to say we are not really creatures at all, but Gods. For all is God if you are a pantheist. That is simply false, for God has created us distinct from himself.

Instead of this, the "nothingness" of the Christian mystic is the nothingness of no self-will and no self-consciousness. "Thy will, not mine, be done" is the fundamental formula for all sanctity, not just that of the mystics. There is nothing particularly mystical about it. But when ravished by God in a foretaste of heaven's beatific vision, the graced mystic also loses all consciousness of himself, he seems to himself to be nothing, because he is no longer looking at himself, only at God. But, of course, he is still there, for there must be a self to exercise the act of self-forgetfulness. Who's forgetting? Not God, surely, for omniscience does not forget.

The Christian mystic experiences a bliss in this total weakness to the point of nothingness, for it is total trust, total relaxing in God's arms, being grasped by Abba, Daddy. All worry and self-concern melt away. This is total humility. As pride is the first sin, the demonic sin, so humility is the first virtue.

Pride does not mean an exaggerated opinion of your own worth; that is vanity. Pride means playing God, demanding to be God. "Better to reign in hell than serve in heaven," says Satan, justifying his rebellion, in Milton's *Paradise Lost*. That is the formula for pride. Pride is the total "my will be done."

Humility is "thy will be done." Humility is focused on God, not self. Humility is not an exaggeratedly low opinion of yourself. Humility is self-forgetfulness. A humble man never tells you how bad he is. He's too busy thinking about *you* to talk about himself. That's why humility is such a joy and so close to the beatific vision, where we will be so fascinated with God that we forget ourselves completely, like the mystics.

Combining these two things—the will's total "not my will but thine be done" and the mind's total self-forgetfulness—we can perhaps begin to understand how the mystics find incomparable joy in becoming nothing. It is the mysterious thrill we feel when we sing to the Holy Spirit, "Blow, blow, blow till I be/ But the breath of the Spirit blowing in me."

It is very hard to talk about this, about ecstasy. It sounds silly sometimes. It is easily misunderstood. It cannot be explained in ordinary language. It is like being in love. It *is* being in love. It is not an idea, to be explained. It is an experience, to be lived, or at least empathized with, open-mindedly and open-heartedly.

How is the cross related to this? In addition to saving us from sin, the cross manifested the nature of God's Trinitarian ecstasy, the Spirit of self-giving love between Father and Son, the very secret of God's inner life. The cross which God planted like a sword in the earth of Calvary was held by the hilt in heaven. Heaven forged its blade. The cross made war on sin and death in time, but it expressed peace and life in eternity.

"Thy will, not mine, be done" is not only the hardest thing we can do (that is what sin has done to us), but it is also the most joyful and liberating thing we can do (that is what grace has offered us). A trillion experiments have proved one point over and over past all doubt: That whenever we aim at happiness as if we were God, by exerting our power and control, we end up in unhappiness, whether we get the thing we wanted or not. For if we get it, we are bored; and if we do not, we are frustrated. But whenever we become nothing, become utterly weak, whenever we say and mean with our whole heart, "Not my will but thine be done," we find the greatest happiness, joy, and peace that is ever possible in this world. Yet despite the trillions of experimental confirmations of this truth, we keep trying other experiments with happiness outside of God and outside of submission to God, thereby repeatedly selling our birthright of joy. In other words, we are insane. Sin is insanity.

The heart of Islam is the powerful truth we have just seen. "Islam" means two things: "submission" and "peace" (cognate with "shalom"). Submission to God ("Allah," "The One") is the way to peace. Dante put it into five words in a line T.S. Eliot called the most perfect and profound line in all literature: "In his will, our peace."

This weakness is the very power of God, the secret of God's omnipotence. God is not omnipotent because he can create a universe or perform miracles. God is omnipotent because he is love, because he can yield to himself, because he can be weak. No theist but a Christian understands the secret of omnipotence. A God who is only one cannot be totally omnipotent. Only the Trinity, only the God who can continually empty himself to himself, can be omnipotent.

We usually think of the Father as the source of omnipotence, but all three persons are necessary for omnipotence. Omnipotence arises only when we come to the Spirit, who *is* the love between Father and Son for each other. When this Spirit enters us, the whole Trinity enters us, and lives his life in and through us. The glorious cross of the eternal Trinity and the bloody cross of Calvary mingle in our souls and lives as we participate in the joy of divine love and in the suffering of divine redemption.

PART SEVEN

The Spiritual War

THIRTY-THREE

A Defense of Fanaticism

Modern society's deepest insult and the new F-word is now "fanatic." A second is "fundamentalist." The media habitually uses these two F-words to describe (or rather demean and denounce) the church's disagreement with their lifestyles of decadence. That is why they will never portray orthodox Catholicism sympathetically. For them, as Fr. George Rutler says, "the only good Catholic is a bad Catholic," a moral "dissenter." When our government judged that a cult leader in Waco was a fanatic and a fundamentalist, they went in with guns blazing on the flimsiest of legal pretexts, risking and sacrificing lives. Christians of the twenty-first century, beware.

Four groups are singled out as the worst offenders: orthodox Catholics, evangelical Protestants (including real fundamentalists), Orthodox Jews, and Muslims. The reason is obvious: These are the only four groups left in the Western world who have not surrendered to the new morality of "free" sex and abortion, who have not bowed the knee to Aphrodite and Moloch.

The aggressively secularistic media hate "fanaticism" because they fear it. They fear it because they envy it. They envy it because it has what they lack and long for: passion. Its passion is deep, honest, and infinite. All four groups preach and practice fanatical, passionate, unlimited love of God and loyalty and obedience to him. They believe in a God who is fully real, objectively true, absolutely good, alarmingly present, and uncontrollably alive—and totally adorable. So they adore.

They also believe and teach that this God is a righteous *judge*, not just an abstract *ideal* or "value." Secularists fear, deep down, that this God may really exist after all, and that therefore they are missing out on the single most important thing in life, as well as probably being on the road to eternal damnation. After all, they know, deep down, that they have no way of being *sure* this God is not there. So they go ballistic when they see a saint, even a little one.

They also get passionate about passion. They have to prove themselves, prove that they aren't what they really are: spiritual wimps. So they substitute sexual passion for religious passion, and become so fanatical about their addiction to it that they practice, justify, and encourage *anything*, from sodomy to baby-killing, to preserve this "right." Nearly all the passion behind abortion comes from sex. If the seventh commandment were obeyed, the fifth would be too. Most murders in America stem from fornication. (Over 99 percent of all murders today are abortions.)

Two current writers, Paul Johnson, in *Intellectuals*, and E. Michael Jones, in *Degenerate Moderns*, have documented the fact that most typically modern ideology stems from sexual deviants and deviance. Sir Julian Huxley, the world's most famous biologist and evolutionist, freely admitted on public radio that the reason natural selection was gobbled up by both scientists and the public as soon as Darwin served it up, was that "it got rid of God, and God was a great bother to our sex life."

How does this apply to us Catholics today in our ordinary daily lives?

We have the fanaticism they lack. We know that the true value of life is very simple. We learn this when someone we love dies. Then, money and fame and even sex simply don't matter any more. Fanatics are "simplistic." Chesterton says, "Morality is always terribly complicated—to someone without principles." Jesus tells Martha, cutting through her complex worries with scandalously "simplistic" words, that "there is only one thing needful."

That is why the saints have real personalities. The unity of any living being—plant, animal, or human being—comes from a oneness of purpose, a unity of end, goal, or good. If you have "one great love," you are one great person. The two greatest and commonest examples of this total self-giving to one great purpose are religion and marriage—the two things the secular media are hell-bent on destroying.

A unity of purpose is necessary for *sanity*. A hard job for a good purpose is not as exhausting as random, meaningless, purposeless work, or working for nothing. The exhaustion of peasants does not kill the human spirit; the boredom of sophisticates does.

What happens when you lose your fanaticism, your passion, your unity of purpose, your absolutes, your meaning of life? You turn into a reptile. Reptiles (1) devour their young, (2) are cold-blooded, and (3) conform their body temperature to the environment. Secularists abort their children. Secularists judge Christians as "fanatics" because to the cold-blooded, a temperature of 98.6 degrees is a high fever. And secularists conform to the environment like good relativists, since they have no objective, unchanging, transcendent, absolute standard to conform to. Modern man is evolving into a reptile.

What can we do?

Our private walk with God can and should respond to this public crisis. For the private and the public aspects of the spiritual life include each other. Each private life is included in the common public life, and public responsibility is included among the responsibilities of each private individual.

But what can we do?

1. I think God wants us to keep our fanaticism hot and healthy. Satan's strategy is to turn us into wimps, to shame us out of fanaticism, that is, obedience to the very first and greatest commandment, to love God with *all* your heart, soul, mind, and strength.
2. I think we should expect even more hysteria, hatred, media lies, injustice, and persecution. The fifties were not normal; the forties and sixties were. Physical or spiritual war is our normal state.
3. I think we should pray for the souls of our persecutors, but also thank God that we have not compromised so much that we are no longer hated. Remember who said, "Woe unto you when all men speak well of you, for so they did of the false prophets." To belong to this Lord is to share his holy unrespectability. It is a necessary part of his cross. If we refuse it, we refuse him. "Anyone who is ashamed of me and my words before men, of him I will be ashamed before my Father."
4. I think we should *rejoice* if we are counted worthy to suffer injustice and hatred for Christ's sake. I think so because Christ said so. However strange that sounds and however hard that is to do, Christ said it.
5. I think we should thank God every day of our lives for his gift of fanaticism. When we love him like crazy, beyond measure and reason, that is his grace, not our achievement. He builds that holy fire in us. If you don't have it but want it, ask him for it and he will give it.

But please don't confuse it with emotion or noise. A loud-mouthed bully and professional prostitute like Madonna is not a fanatic. A quiet, humble *woman* like *the* Madonna is. Indeed, she was the most fanatical mere-human who ever lived.

And don't confuse it with narrowness. The saints, who are the most "fanatic" and "simplistic," are also the most fascinatingly flexible, unpredictably individual, and creatively original about everything else except inventing new gods. On the other hand, the secularists, lacking an absolute, will inevitably absolutize and fixate on something relative, like sex, sodomy, abortion, or "freedom." (C.S. Lewis writes, with heady liberation, "I was not born to be free. I was born to adore and to obey.") Such fixated secularists become increasingly narrow, rigid, shrill, and closed-minded about their gods.

Saints—true fanatics—are secularists' only hope. When they see a saint, they will either freeze or melt—either get even more rigid with hate and fear or melt with longing. Sometimes they will do both at the same time, with different parts of their soul. It is not our business to know what they do. Our eyes are not to be on them, or on ourselves, but on Christ. He is the model fanatic, who did what we must do. He ignored and disobeyed those, even his own disciples, who said they would believe in him and accept him if only he were less fanatical. Instead, he kept his eyes and his heart on his Father's will alone. By doing the same, his disciples turned the world upside down. Today the world is turning us upside down. The key to reversing that process and reconverting the world is simple ("simplistic"): a return to the fanaticism of sanctity, the fanaticism of Mary's "fiat," the fanaticism of "the first and greatest commandment," the fanaticism of the way of the cross.

THIRTY-FOUR

The Six Things We Need to Know to Save the World

Our world is dying, and we need to know just six things to save it.

1. The immediate and obvious problem is social decay. If our ancestors could see our society, they would be dismayed and discombobulated. We are increasingly becoming a society of dumbed-down, drugged-out, divorced killers, abusers, rapists, sodomites, catamites, and spiritual termites. Trust, happiness, fidelity, families, privacy, and personality are all festering faster and faster.

   The problems have not gone away despite increased government money, programs, and education. Nor will they. No amount of money, no political structures, and no "value-free education" has ever done or will ever do anything but exacerbate all the problems.

   The only solution is moral, and everybody knows it—*except*

those in charge of our money, our politics, our law, our schools, and our mind-molding media.

2. Social morality, however, depends on individual morality—on character, not on structures; on virtue, not on politics. A team, or an army, or a school, or a community is a good one if and only if its individuals are good people, just as a brick wall is a good wall only if the bricks are good bricks.
3. Morality, in turn, throughout all of human history, has always depended on religion. There has never been a long-range successful secular morality. Paganism, Confucianism, Taoism, Hinduism, Islam, Buddhism, Judaism, and Christianity have been the eight main moral systems that have worked in human history.
4. Religion means some sort of God. The true God is the God of Abraham, the God of the Jews, whom Muslims call Allah (The One) and whom Jesus calls his Father. He claims to be God's Son and says no one can know or come to God except through him. If this is not true, he is the most insanely blasphemous egomaniac who ever lived. If it is true—well, then it is true. That is the essence of Christianity: Christ.
5. Just as we meet God only through Christ, we meet Christ only through his Holy Spirit, not through books or feelings or reasoning or yoga or psychology. The Spirit is the only fuel powerful enough to take you up the holy mountain.
6. Finally, the Spirit is the soul of a visible body, the church. Christ left the church as *his* church. We know about Christ only because the church exists. That is simply a historical fact. The Bible was written, canonized, and used by the church.

The Roman Catholic church claims to be that body in its fullness. Just as with the claims of Christ himself, if this is not true, it is the most blasphemously arrogant claim any church has ever made. If she is not divine, she is demonic.

But if she is demonic, how could she have produced all those saints for two thousand years? Why would Satan inspire a Mother Teresa?

And now we come to you. You can be a Mother Teresa or a Francis. You are a walking advertisement for the Roman Catholic church, and thus for the Holy Spirit, and thus Christ, and thus God, and thus ethics, and thus the salvation of society. You can save the world.

How do you become a saint? By wanting to be. There is no method. There are no buttons to push, no technology, no techniques. It's love. It's the heart.

You can't make yourself a saint, only God can. You can stop him or let him. But that *is* sanctity—letting him. That is its essence.

Sanctity and sin are the only two things that you can do simply by willing it. And one of them saves the world.

THIRTY-FIVE

The World's Last Night

Some day I shall write a philosophical fantasy. I must warn you that the identity of the author of this fantasy is not myself. His identity will be revealed in due time in the course of the story. In this fantasy, everything else will follow logically from one fantastic assumption. The assumption is simply that in this fantasy world everyone has only one absolute: They will have sex however, whenever, and with whomever they will. Sex is the only absolute, intrinsic good. Everything else must fall into line around that.

Now the beings inhabiting this fantasy world would be human, not extraterrestrials. So their psychology would be not fantasy but fact.

Here are three relevant facts about the human psyche:

1. Sex can be addictive.

2. Addictions are imperious and demanding. Each addiction demands to be treated like a god.

3. Addictions blind you. They make you rationalize instead of reason. That is, the mind is used as servant, to justify what is desired, rather than served as master, to seek objective truth.

The will (captain) tells the mind (the navigator) when to speak and what to say.

In my fantasy, I wonder "What if?" If my givens were granted, what would follow? What would such a world be like? How would it rationalize?

First, its moralists and ethicians would abandon the universal moral law, the belief in unyielding and unchangeable absolutes, which was held by every society in history. It might even call this abandonment of the common belief of all cultures "multiculturalism," if it were particularly arrogant about how stupid people were and how easily the Big Lie could be believed.

The morality of such a society would not go beyond compassion—that is, not doing what makes people unhappy (for example, telling them to control their sex drives). At its highest, their morality might attain a golden rule, or Kantian "categorical imperative"—do to others only what you want them to do to you. This would forbid murder (except to those who no longer loved life), and theft (except to socialists), and lying (except to those who did not love or believe in truth), but it would allow seducing to anyone who would like to be seduced. Such a society would invent slogans like "Make love, not war."

Second, it would follow that all previous societies, which believed that sex was sacred and should be surrounded by taboos of some sort, would have to be ignored, dismissed with labels like "unprogressive," or else "reinterpreted" (that is, lied about, but in scholarly ways). Words like "tradition" and "authority," which in all previous societies were reverence words, would have to become sneer words in this one.

Third, since this society would deny the authority and wisdom of the collective experience of the past, it would also deny one of the most massively obvious facts of present as well as past experience: that control of our immediate instincts and desires makes for physical, emotional, and mental health and happiness; and that never resisting them results in addiction and misery, both individually and societally. Its psychology would not be based on experience but ideology.

Fourth, its religion would have to deny the existence of an objective, transcendent God with a will and a moral law. It would have to deny the authority of the Bible, both Old and New Testaments, since this book so crudely and obviously contradicts its chosen "lifestyle." God the Father would be changed into God the Cosmic Chum, God the Wonderful Wimp, or God the Compassionate Compromiser.

It would also have to deny ("nuance" is the word preferred by cowards and scholars) the divinity and infallibility of Christ, who was not sexually "liberated." It would deny his resurrection (evidence for his divinity). The simplest way to do this would be to deny miracles in general. This would also effectively pull God's claws; for a God who could work miracles is also a God who can give a real moral law. "A God we can feel comfortable with" would be infinitely more attractive.

The new religionists in my fantasy would also deny the authority of any church that dared to contradict its "lifestyle." If they claimed membership in a church with a traditional sex ethic, these heretics would be rechristened "progressives." They would concentrate, with monomaniacal obsession, only on sexual themes: divorce, fornication, adultery, feminism, homosexuality, condoms, contraception, abortion, priestesses, sexually inclusive language, and pedophilia. Then they would accuse the *church* of monomaniacal obsession with sex!

Fifth, even biological theory would be pressed into service. Evolution would prove human beings are only animals, and therefore that it is unrealistic to expect them to act with more self-control than a rabbit.

Sixth, the popular mind would interpret even Einstein's physical theory of relativity as a justification of *moral* relativity. They might even seize on Heisenberg's Uncertainty Principle in quantum physics to bolster *moral* skepticism. This could also be derived from Goedel's Theorem in math, thereby giving pseudo-scientific backing for the moral relativism and skepticism that is necessary to justify their sexual obsession.

Seventh, in philosophy post-modernism would replace modernism (rationalism), and deconstructionism would be a fancy name for "anything goes." All restraint would be labelled repressive, regressive, and naïve.

Eighth, even their cosmology would have to reject the common principle of all traditional and common-sensical cosmology, namely hierarchy. For cosmic hierarchy is the rational basis for authority, and authority just might tell us what to do with our sex organs. This must be prevented at all costs—cut off at the pass, so to speak.

Ninth, in politics, the notions of rightful authority and obedience to law would be seen as too similar to the notions of "authority" and "obedience" in morality, so they would be replaced by "rights," "victim" status, "compassion," and "consensus" as the foundational concepts of their social order. The very notion of excellence (excelling, being superior) must be ruthlessly destroyed and called "elitist." The government must systematically reward the less excellent, the less talented, the less successful, and the less moral. It must reward the lazy and the complainer and punish the hardworking and the morally superior, at least economically.

Tenth, a consumerist economics would emerge, which would treat sex as a consumer item. It might treat money as if it were sex, trying to make it pregnant and multiply, and sex as if it were money—something to spend at will.

Before I go any further with details for my fantasy, I should remind you that this whole scenario is a *very* far-fetched fantasy that I expect no one to believe. How could they? How could such a diverse and complete array of social changes all result from one single sexual cause? It's just not believable.

And since this is so, I have just realized that such a story is not worth telling. So I will stop telling this silly story very soon now, before it gets even sillier. Perhaps tonight.

Sincerely yours,
The Creator

THIRTY-SIX

Divorce, Doctors, and Dissent

Lawn mowing can be great mental exercise, and can trim thoughts as well as grass. Just now, behind my lawn mower, I realized the connection between two little events that happened to me today and the larger lesson they contained.

Event one was my reading for the umpteenth time in a student paper, words like these about the church's "rigid stance" against divorce: "The church is not meeting the needs of a changing society. The church is part of the community and must adapt to the needs of the people. The church must change (that is, allow divorce)."

Event two was a telephone conversation with my daughter's doctor. I was about to give her penicillin for a bad sore throat, and my wife wisely told me to check with the doctor first. I called him up, and he said no, the penicillin would more likely do harm than good. I was surprised and registered a mild dissent. He replied gently, "Who's the doctor here?"

The church claims to be the world's spiritual doctor. Either she is, or she isn't. If she isn't, then she's a fake, a quack, and should be run out of town. If she is, then she'd better be listened to and obeyed, even when her orders surprise us—*especially* when her orders surprise us. After all, "Who's the doctor here?"

"Dissenters"—liberals, modernists, revisionists—are not usually bad people. They usually have good motives. They usually have a good motive for wanting the church to "adapt" to the world. The motive is to be *helpful*; they want the church to be helpful to people in modern times. But the church can't be helpful by adapting her teachings to the world's opinions any more than the doctor can be helpful by adapting his advice to the patient's opinions.

Only a doctor who is right where the patient is wrong is helpful. A doctor who is right when the patient is right is not helpful, only harmless. A doctor who is wrong when the patient is wrong is not helpful but helpless. And a doctor who is wrong when the patient is right is not helpful but harmful.

Only a church that is right when the world is wrong is helpful. A church that is right when the world is right is not helpful, only harmless. A church that is wrong when the world is wrong is not helpful but helpless. And a church that is wrong when the world is right is not helpful but harmful.

I respect the mind of a consistent atheist like Marx or Voltaire, who says the church should be destroyed, more than the mind of a "dissenting" Catholic who says the church should "adapt" its teachings to the world's opinion polls. Either the church or the world is wrong (unless the Law of Non-Contradiction has been repealed). If the world is wrong, it had better repent and right itself by following Doctor Church. If the church is wrong, she ought to be run out of town as a quack.

The ultimate reason why the church *can't* "adapt" to the world is that her founder guaranteed her that the gates of the place the world is going to will never prevail against her.

THIRTY-SEVEN

Endings

As we approach the end of a decade and of a millennium, it is a natural time for reflections about endings—a sort of seventh-inning stretch in the baseball game of history.

I said *reflections*, not *predictions*. We are wise, I think, to let the fundamentalists corner the market in predictions about the end-time scenario. Since Christ himself didn't know when he was coming again (Mt 24:36), it seems unbelievably brash for us to try to upstage him.

I have never understood the fundamentalist fascination with details of the Second Coming. Perhaps it attracts us as a pleasant and effective diversion from present duties. That would give some ground for the Marxists' gibe about religion being the "opiate of the people." In fact *politics*—not religion—is the opiate of the people.

But if he may come at any time, he may come this decade, this year, this night. Any night could be the world's last night, and the decade we are now entering may well be the world's last decade. There would be a kind of fittingness to such an end, if we judge by biblical numerology. Archbishop Ussher's literal (and factually mistaken) calculating of Old Testament genealogies gave him 4004 B.C. as the date of the creation of the world, and Christ's first coming was in 4 B.C., exactly 4,000 years later. Scripture says that a thousand years are as one day to God, and one day as a thousand years (Ps 90:4). So the seventh millennium, which would be God's seventh day, the eternal sabbath, would be due to begin in A.D. 1996. But I doubt the world will end in 1996, simply because too many people expect it, and one thing we do know about it is that it will be unexpected, like a thief in the night (Mt 24:4).

The Holy Father has called these last years of our millennium an "advent time." History seems about to turn some great corner. But what corner?

Without pretending to choose between them, I see three likely futures for the next millennium, if there *is* a next millennium:

1. It may well be that our civilization is dying as Rome was dying in Augustine's time. If so, let us not cry over spilt milk or spoiled garbage. If we don't know that our primary citizenship is in the undying city of God rather than in the doomed and dying city of the world, we'd better read Augustine's great classic *The City of God* (or, better and simpler, Scripture).

2. Or it may be that we shall stay alive as a spiritual corpse, drifting into *A Brave New World*, without war but also without passion—without poverty or starvation, but with terrible *spiritual* poverty and starvation instead. But such a world, I think, would be unstable and could not last very long. A society of total self-indulgence even to the extent of swallowing its own children, like Moloch, cannot last much longer than "The Thousand-Year Reich." In this world, at least, holocausts never last forever. Thus this second possibility for the future goes over into the first one, and our reaction to it also: good riddance to bad rubbish.

3. Or perhaps the coming century will be "the Christian century." The liberal journal by that name was founded in 1900 with that naïve prediction. More realistic would seem to be the vision of Pope Leo XIII that God gave the devil one century and he chose the twentieth. Well, perhaps the worst is over. Perhaps the addict—self-addicted secular society—is about to hit bottom and bounce back, that is, repent. In a world which has already tried every revolution and every radicalism, orthodoxy is the only possible revolution of tomorrow.

We do not and we need not know which scenario awaits us, for our duties and our hopes are identical in all three: to love God with our whole heart and soul and mind and strength, and our neighbor as ourselves. For if our society is doomed, our souls are not. No society lasts forever, anymore than any body lasts forever. But when this civilization, and this millennium, and this planet, and the very stars, have all long died, you and I will still be just beginning, always beginning. As the famous hymn "Amazing Grace" puts it:

When we've been there ten thousand years,
Bright shining like the sun,
We've no less days to sing God's praise
Than when we've first begun.

Scripture says that a way to attain wisdom is to "number our days," to know that our days are numbered (Ps 90:12). The effect on our lives of this remembering of death—individual, civilizational, and universal—is exactly the opposite of morbidity or escapism. C.S. Lewis says it perfectly in his essay, "The Weight of Glory":

It is a serious thing to live in a society of possible gods and goddesses, to remember that the dullest and most uninteresting person you can talk to may one day be a creature which, if you saw it now, you would be strongly tempted to worship, or else a horror and a corruption such as you now meet, if at all, only in a nightmare. All day long we are, in some degree, helping each other to one or other of these destinations.... You have never talked to a mere mortal. Nations, cultures, arts, civilizations—these are mortal, and their life is to ours as the life of a gnat. But it is immortals whom we joke with, work with, marry, snub, and exploit—immortal horrors or everlasting splendours.